USING ADMINISTRATIVE DATA TO STRENGTHEN DEVELOPMENT STATISTICS IN ASIA AND THE PACIFIC

NOVEMBER 2023

ASIAN DEVELOPMENT BANK

Contents

Tables, Figures, and Boxes

Foreword

National statistical systems (NSSs) play a critical role in compiling data for development. They consist of national statistics offices and other government institutions that collect, process, and disseminate official statistics used by policymakers and development practitioners. In developing Asian economies, these institutions typically rely on conventional methods like sample surveys and censuses to compile data on demographics, economics, employment, and poverty, among other development topics.

The 2030 Agenda for Sustainable Development calls for a "data revolution," as it aims to provide more timely, granular, and accurate data. Making such data widely available remains a challenge for NSSs because of the cost and considerable resources associated with conventional methods of data production. The data revolution entails integrating multiple sources of data for the purpose of enhancing granularity, timeliness, and accuracy of information derived from using only one type of data.

Data from administrative records, originally intended for regulatory purposes or government programs, offer a valuable source of information that can complement surveys and censuses. Administrative data may potentially enhance statistical quality and reduce costs when integrated with other types of data, such as those coming from surveys and censuses. By harnessing administrative data that are routinely collected, surveys and censuses can be streamlined to achieve larger sample sizes and enhanced timeliness at a lower cost, offering significant advantages, especially in contexts wherein NSSs confront budgetary constraints.

The lockdowns that were enforced during the coronavirus disease (COVID-19) pandemic tremendously disrupted the operations of NSSs, posing an additional challenge to the conduct of conventional surveys and censuses, which are frequently used to compile development statistics, including Sustainable Development Goal (SDG) indicators. These traditional data collection activities typically require face-to-face interactions in the field. Harnessing administrative data helped facilitate "data resilience," which is the uninterrupted flow of information despite the difficulty experienced during the collection, compilation, and analyses of data.

In the labor sector, administrative data provide a rich source of information for monitoring employment patterns. When combined with other types of data, administrative records can meet the disaggregated data requirements for select SDG indicators on employment, including information on social protection coverage and social security benefits (SDG indicator 1.3.1) and data on occupational injuries (SDG indicator 8.8.1). The availability of granular data on work- and employment-related indicators helps ensure that no one is left behind in the implementation of the 2030 Agenda for Sustainable Development.

Challenges in using administrative data for the compilation of development indicators also exist. For instance, administrative data are not initially designed for statistical use. Furthermore, existing laws on data confidentiality may restrain the use of administrative data.

In 2018, the Asian Development Bank (ADB) approved the Data for Development (Phase 2) technical assistance (TA) project, which was designed to enhance the statistical capacity of the NSSs of selected ADB's developing member economies in Asia and the Pacific. This TA is linked to the Global Action Plan for Sustainable

Development Data through SDG target 17.19, which supports statistical capacity building in developing economies. The TA project is also aligned with the draft framework of ADB's Strategy 2030, wherein both the developing member economies and ADB have pledged support to the SDGs and the related Financing for Development agenda. In the long run, this TA supports the SDGs through technological advances and capacity building across five domains, including quality labor statistics using data integration principles.

This report on using administrative data in the compilation of employment-related and other socioeconomic indicators is produced at a time when the demand for data-driven policies that can advance labor market outcomes is high. Establishing that administrative data can provide a wealth of information that can be used in the labor sector, this report presents insights into the wide range of ways in which administrative data can be used to provide more nuanced and timely insights for designing policies that aim to improve workers' condition.

This report was prepared by the Statistics and Data Innovation Unit (EROD-SDI) under the Economic Research and Development Impact Department (ERDI), coordinated by Arturo Martinez Jr. under the overall direction of Elaine Tan. Jose Ramon Albert, who prepared the first draft of the report, and Margarita Guerrero, who later led the enhancement of the report, served as the main authors of this report. Arturo Martinez Jr., Joseph Albert Nino Bulan, Rose Anne Dumayas, Remedios Espineda, Marymell Martillan, Mildred Addawe, and Christian Flora Mae Soco coauthored some sections of the report and provided technical and coordination support in preparing the report.

The preparation of this report was made possible because of the support, assistance, and cooperation extended by the statistical partners in developing member economies throughout the Asia and Pacific region and the invaluable contributions of international organizations. The input that came from several developing member economies through their responses to the Survey on the Use of Administrative Data for the Compilation of Employment-Related Indicators conducted by the EROD-SDI constitutes a significant part of this report. Government partners from a few developing member economies participated in the focus group discussions that became an avenue for a more thorough discussion of the topic of interest. These partners included the Statistical Committee of the Republic of Armenia, the Ministry of Labor and Social Affairs of Armenia, the National Statistical Office of Mongolia, and the Ministry of Labor and Social Protection of Mongolia. Colleagues from various Government of Singapore agencies collaborated to prepare the consolidated written responses to the focus group discussion questions. These agencies included the Department of Statistics, Ministry of Manpower, Accounting and Corporate Regulatory Authority, Enterprise Singapore, Immigration & Checkpoints Authority, Ministry of Health, Singapore Food Agency, Ministry of Education, and Infocomm Media Development Authority. The ADB report team is highly appreciative of the United Nations Economic and Social Commission for Asia and the Pacific (ESCAP) for providing the platform to solicit feedback from the members of Data Integration Community of Practice coordinated by ESCAP. The ADB report team is especially grateful to ESCAP's Afsaneh Yazdani, who helped share the manuscript in ESCAP's platform and for helping with coordination. The report team also appreciates the input of colleagues from the International Labour Organization and participants in the Data for Development (Phase 2) Dissemination workshop.

Jason Beerman copyedited the manuscript, Francis Manio prepared the cover design and some infographics, Alfredo De Jesus did the typesetting, and Marjorie Celis did the page proof review.

Albert Park
Chief Economist and Director General
Economic Research and Development Impact Department
Asian Development Bank

Abbreviations

ADB	Asian Development Bank
COVID-19	coronavirus disease
ESDC	Employment Insurance Statistics program from Employment and Social Development Canada
FSP	Food Stamp Program
IDI	Integrated Data Infrastructure
ILO	International Labour Organization
LFS	labor force survey
LSMS	living standards measurement survey
NSS	national statistical system
NSO	national statistics office
OECD	Organisation for Economic Co-operation and Development
SDG	Sustainable Development Goal
SUADCEI	Survey on the Use of Administrative Data for the Compilation of Employment-Related Indicators
UNECE	United Nations Economic Commission for Europe
UNESCAP	United Nations Economic and Social Commission for Asia and the Pacific
UNSD	United Nations Statistics Division

Overview

I. Introduction

As economies seek insights on how labor markets operate, and how programs and policies affect labor market outcomes, they draw information from trends in work, unemployment, labor utilization, and other work-related indicators. These insights feed into an economy's jobs agenda as articulated in their medium- and long-term national development plans.

At the global level, work-related development, in the context of leaving-no-one-behind articulated in the 2030 Agenda for Sustainable Development and Sustainable Development Goal (SDG) 8, which emphasizes that economies need to "promote sustained, inclusive and sustainable economic growth, full and productive employment and decent work for all." Achieving this SDG involves carrying out several actions at the economy-level, including protection of workers' rights, attainment of gender-balanced working arrangements, eradication of precarious and prohibited forms of work such as child labor; and increased social protection coverage among the most vulnerable segments of the labor force.

With time-bound targets, the monitoring of progress in attaining the desired outcomes through objective measures is essential, and measures based on granular and timely data and statistics are needed for this purpose.

Context: Labor Policy, Sustainable Development Goal Targets, and Monitoring Indicators

While this report focuses on the statistical aspects of why and how monitoring indicators can be produced from administrative data systems, it has to be stated that the importance of this work comes from the policy outcomes that the indicators are intended for.

Results from the Asian Development Bank (ADB) Survey on the Use of Administrative Data for the Compilation of Employment-Related Indicators (SUADCEI) 2022c (Box 1) reveal the extent to which administrative data have been used to design labor and economic policies as well as policies relating to education, health, and social protection. Specifically, 13 national statistics offices (NSOs) and 7 labor and social ministries stated that other government offices use the administrative data that they collect in the development of labor policies while 13 NSOs and 5 labor and social ministries claimed that the administrative data that they collect are used in designing economic policies (Figure 1).

**Box 1: Survey on the Use of Administrative Data for the Compilation
of Employment-related Indicators 2022**

The Survey on the Use of Administrative Data for the Compilation of Employment-Related
Indicators, conducted by the Statistics and Data Innovation Unit of the Economic Research
and Development Impact Department of the Asian Development Bank (ADB), asked
questions about ADB regional members' experiences in using administrative data in the
context of compiling work and employment-related indicators.

A total of 24 national statistics offices, 8 labor ministries, and 4 social welfare ministries
from 27 ADB members participated in the survey: Armenia; Azerbaijan; Bangladesh; Bhutan;
Brunei Darussalam; Cambodia; the Cook Islands; Fiji; Georgia; Hong Kong, China; Indonesia;
Kazakhstan; Malaysia; the Marshall Islands; Mongolia; Nauru; Nepal; Pakistan; the Philippines;
Samoa; Singapore; Sri Lanka; Thailand; Timor-Leste; Tonga; Uzbekistan; and Viet Nam. Data
collection took place from October 2021 to February 2022.

Questionnaires are found in the appendixes.

Source: ADB. 2022a. *Key Indicators for Asia and the Pacific 2022.* Manila. https://www.adb.org/sites/default/
files/publication/812946/ki2022.pdf.

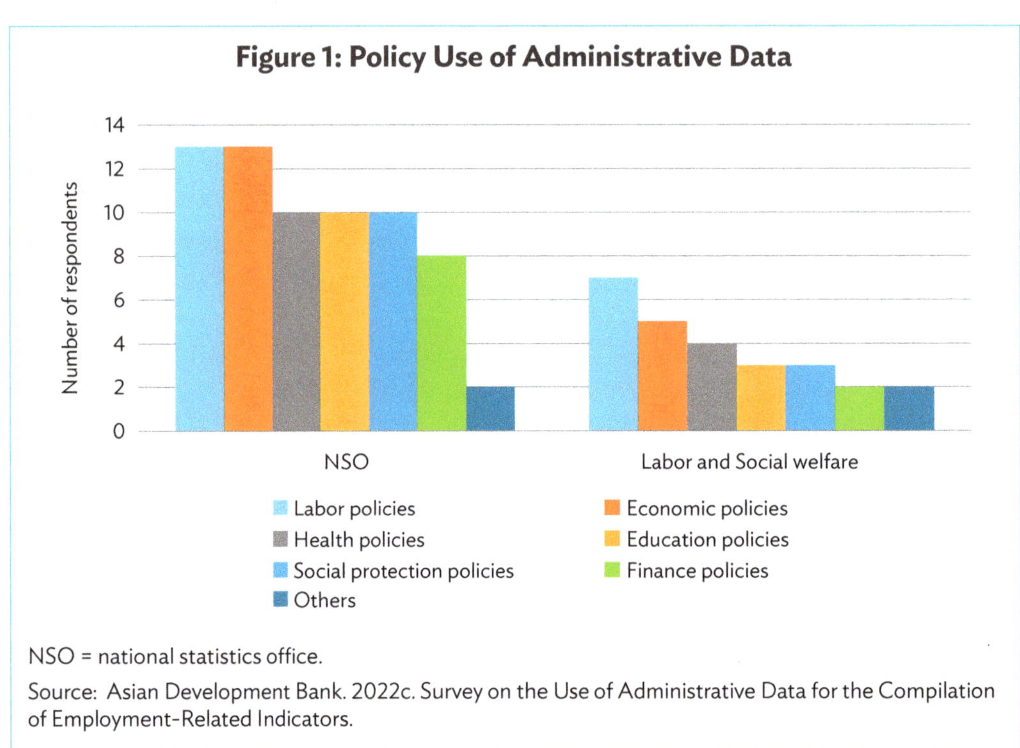

Figure 1: Policy Use of Administrative Data

NSO = national statistics office.
Source: Asian Development Bank. 2022c. Survey on the Use of Administrative Data for the Compilation
of Employment-Related Indicators.

A useful organizing framework, developed by the International Labour Organization (ILO), for linking desired
policy outcomes on decent work for sustainable development to thematic areas of work and to the relevant SDG
goals and targets is illustrated in Table 1 and Table 2.

Table 1: Policy Outcomes and Related Thematic Areas of Work

Policy Outcomes	Thematic Areas
1. More and better jobs for inclusive growth and improved youth prospects 2. Ratification and application of international labor standards 3. Creating and extending social protection floors 4. Promoting sustainable enterprises 5. Decent work in the rural economy 6. Formalization of the informal economy 7. Promoting workplace compliance through labor inspection 8. Promoting workers from unacceptable forms of work 9. Promoting fair and effective labor migration policies 10. Strong and representative employers' and workers' organizations	1. Active labor market policies 2. Child labor 3. Employment-rich economic growth 4. Enterprise development 5. Environment and green jobs 6. Equality 7. Forced labor 8. Freedom of association and collective bargaining 9. Future of work 10. Gender equality and non-discrimination 11. Global supply chains 12. Health and safety at the workplace 13. Informal economy 14. Labor market information systems 15. Labor migration 16. Labor standards 17. National employment policies 18. Productivity 19. Rural economy 20. Skills and employability 21. Social dialogue and tripartism 22. Social protection floor 23. Working conditions 24. Youth employment

Sources: International Labour Organization. Decent work for sustainable development Resource Platform: Policy Outcomes. https://www.ilo.org/global/topics/dw4sd/theme-by-policy-outcomes/lang--en/index.htm; and ILO. Decent work for sustainable development Resource Platform: Thematic areas. https://www.ilo.org/global/topics/dw4sd/themes/lang--en/index.htm.

Table 2: Mapping Thematic Areas and Decent Work Policy Outcomes: Illustrations

Thematic Area	Policy Outcome (refer to Table 1)	SDG Targets[a]
Active labor market policies	1, 2, 3, 4, 6, 10	1.5, 8.5, 8.8, 9.a, 9.b
Child labor	2, 8, 10	8.7, 16.2
Equality	1, 3, 7, 8	8.8, 10.1, 10.3, 10.4
Gender equality and nondiscrimination	1, 2, 3, 6, 7, 8, 10	1.4, 4.5, 5.2, 5.4, 5.5, 5.a, 8.5, 8.8, 10.3
Health and safety at the workplace	2, 6, 7, 8, 10	3.9, 8.8, 16.6
Informal economy	6	8.3, 10.2
Rural economy	5	1.2, 2.3, 8.2
Youth employment	1, 10	4.4, 8.5, 8.6, 8.b

ILO = International Labour Organization, SDG = Sustainable Development Goal.

[a] Documentation on SDG targets for each of the 17 goals is provided on various online platforms, including United Nations, Department of Economic and Social Affairs. The 17 Goals. https://sdgs.un.org/goals.

Sources: ILO. Decent work for sustainable development Resource Platform: Policy Outcomes. https://www.ilo.org/global/topics/dw4sd/theme-by-policy-outcomes/lang--en/index.htm; and ILO. Decent work for sustainable development Resource Platform: Thematic areas. https://www.ilo.org/global/topics/dw4sd/themes/lang--en/index.htm.

With this organizing framework, the links between policy outcomes, SDG targets, and the associated monitoring indicators as well as other labor-related indicators can be made. This is illustrated in Table 3.

Table 3: Indicators for Gender Equality and Discrimination

Thematic Area	Policy Outcome (refer to Table 1)	SDG Targets
Gender equality and nondiscrimination	1, 2, 3, 6, 7, 8, 10	1.4, 4.5, 5.2, 5.4, 5.5, 5.a, 8.5, 8.8, 10.3

SDG indicators:[a]

1.1.1   Proportion of population below the international poverty line, by sex, age, employment status and geographical location (urban or rural)

2.3.2   Average income of small-scale food producers, by sex and indigenous status

4.5.1   Parity indices (female/male, rural/urban, bottom/top wealth quintile and others such as disability status, indigenous peoples and conflict-affected, as data become available) for all education indicators on this list that can be disaggregated

5.4.1   Proportion of time spent on unpaid domestic and care work, by sex, age and location

5.5.2   Proportion of women in managerial positions

8.3.1   Proportion of informal employment in non-agriculture employment, by sex

8.5.1   Average hourly earnings of female and male employees, by occupation, age and persons with disabilities

8.5.2   Unemployment rate, by sex, age and persons with disabilities

8.8.1   Frequency rates of fatal and nonfatal occupational injuries, by sex and migrant status

Other indicators:
Employment-to-population ratio by sex and age
Hours of work by sex and economic activity
Labor force participation rate by sex and age
Vulnerable employment rate by sex

ILO = International Labour Organization, SDG = Sustainable Development Goal.

[a]   Information on SDG indicators are regularly updated at United Nations Statistics Division. SDG Indicators. https://unstats.un.org/sdgs/indicators/indicators-list/.

Sources: ILO. Decent work for sustainable development Resource Platform: Thematic areas—Gender Equality and Non-Discrimination. https://www.ilo.org/global/topics/dw4sd/themes/gender-equality/lang--en/index.htm. and ILO. Decent work for sustainable development Resource Platform: Thematic areas—Gender Equality and Non-Discrimination, Indicators for Gender Equality and Non-Discrimination. https://www.ilo.org/global/topics/dw4sd/themes/gender-equality/WCMS_560718/lang--en/index.htm.

Why Focus on Administrative Data

(i)   Work and labor market-related indicators are produced from multiple data streams. For the compilation of official statistics and indicators, institutions of national statistical systems collect input data from various sources. Traditional sources of data such as surveys and censuses are time-consuming, labor intensive, and expensive, and they pose a reporting burden for respondents. Official statistics producers are therefore increasingly using or exploring the use of other data sources, including big data, geospatial information, citizen-generated data, and administrative data and records (Box 2). The movement toward expanding data sources holds for the production of statistics and indicators about labor markets.

Box 2: What Are Administrative Data?

The United Nations' Fundamental Principles of Official Statistics state that "Data for statistical purposes may be drawn from all types of sources, be they statistical surveys or administrative records."

Examples of administrative records are records of members, activities, or individuals relevant to mandates of agencies or institutions. These records consist of variables associated with units and unit identifiers created for administrative purposes.

The term "administrative data" refers here to data found in administrative records collected by a government ministry, department, or agency primarily for administrative (not research or statistical) purposes. These administrative purposes are related to the corresponding executive or lawful functions such as authorizations, registrations, permits, payments, sanctions, and control. Administrative data may include both data in administrative registers and data in other administrative sources.

Source: United Nations Statistics Division. 2022. *Handbook on Management and Organization of National Statistical Systems*. New York (section 8.3: Administrative sources). https://unstats.un.org/capacity-development/handbook/Handbook_20230417.pdf.

(ii)   Administrative data systems and the records they maintain have specific infrastructure, processes, and outputs that serve the agency's purpose. Processes in an administrative data system typically involve registration, transaction, and record keeping which derive data as by-products. Examples include

    (a)   health, pension, and employment data in a social security system;
    (b)   income or expenditure records of tax authorities;
    (c)   data on registered unemployment, active labor market programs, and social benefits from a social protection program; and
    (d)   labor inspection records pertaining to occupational injuries.

(iii)   It has already been established that administrative data can serve as useful supplementary source of information for monitoring international and national development targets (ADB 2010; United Nations Economic and Social Commission for Asia and the Pacific [UNESCAP] 2019; United Nations Economic Commission for Europe [UNECE] 2020).

The SUADCEI provides information on how NSOs and labor and social ministries use administrative data (Figure 2). Among the list of possible uses, NSOs use administrative data mainly for statistical purposes, while labor and social ministries use administrative data for service delivery.

Administrative data can be harnessed to add value to an economy's labor market information system. A business register,[1] linked with a tax register, for example, can be used to help inform policymakers about how many businesses in different sectors are still open and how many have shut down following the coronavirus disease (COVID-19) pandemic. These linked data sources can provide information on the number of employees before and during the pandemic, to describe the impact of the pandemic on the economy. If these sources are further linked to health registers, they can provide an extra mechanism for contact tracing in case infections may have occurred in places of work.

---

[1]   A register is typically a structured list of units (say people or businesses) containing a number of attributes for each of those units, and having some sort of regular updating mechanism (UNECE 2011).

Specific instances of the use of administrative data in the absence of other data sources during the COVID-19 pandemic are described in Box 3.

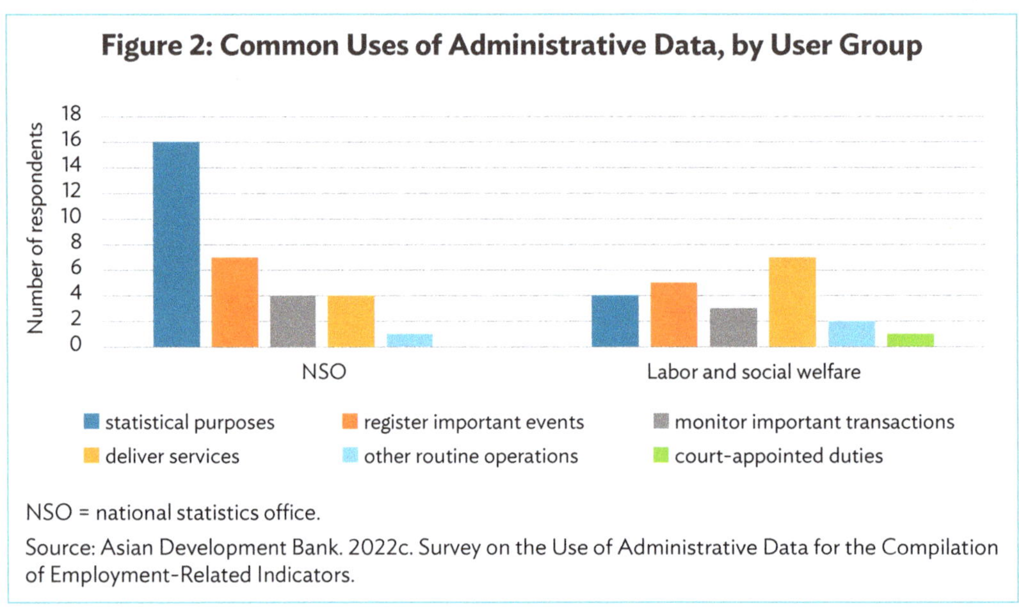

Figure 2: Common Uses of Administrative Data, by User Group

NSO = national statistics office.
Source: Asian Development Bank. 2022c. Survey on the Use of Administrative Data for the Compilation of Employment-Related Indicators.

Box 3: Administrative Data Sources Come to the Rescue

When the coronavirus disease (COVID-19) pandemic struck, administrative data systems were used to generate timely profiles of health conditions as seen from daily aggregate data on new infections, recoveries, and deaths from COVID-19. Administrative data collected from persons and businesses were also used to monitor the impacts of the pandemic and to set up mechanisms for social assistance.

For example, Samoa's Ministry of Commerce, Industry and Labour used administrative data for conducting a rapid assessment on conditions of businesses and workers in the wake of the pandemic.[a]

The Philippines' Department of Labor and Employment, together with other government agencies, have used workers' data registers linked with tax records to provide financial assistance for displaced workers.[b]

In Malaysia, the Department of Statistics has linked administrative data from the Employees' Provident Fund and the Inland Revenue Board (which covers 70%–80% of the population) and with the resulting data provided policymakers a timely portrait of how the COVID-19 pandemic had affected the labor market.[c]

Sources:

[a]   Asian Development Bank. 2022c. Survey on the Use of Administrative Data for the Compilation of Employment-Related Indicators.

[b]   Government of the Philippines, *Department of Labor and Employment. 2020. Department Order No. 12: Prescribing Guidelines on the Provision of Financial Assistance for Displaced Landbased and Seabased Filipino Workers Due to the Corona Virus Disease (COVID-19).* Manila. https://www.dole.gov.ph/news/department-order-no-212-series-of-2020-prescribing-guidelines-on-the-provision-of-financial-assistance-for-displaced-landbased-and-seabased-filipino-workers-due-to-the-corona-virus-covid-2019-d/.

[c]   F.C. Soco, et al. 2021a. Harnessing Administrative Data for Evidence-Based Policy-Making. Development Asia. *Development Asia.* Manila: https://development.asia/insight/harnessing-administrative-data-evidence-based-labor-policy-making.

II. How to Use This Report

Objectives of This Report

This report looks at statistics and indicators that are used to formulate and monitor implementation and outcomes of work-related policies. This is intended to serve as a knowledge resource that (i) explains why administrative records and the data that they generate, i.e., administrative data, should be utilized in producing these statistics and indicators; and (ii) provides practical guidance through examples on how this can be efficiently done. The guidance draws on outcomes and lessons learned from national and international initiatives that have come up with solutions to the issues challenges in using administrative data to produce official statistics as applied to the generation of statistics and indicator values on work. The presentations in this document focus, in particular, on the employment and work-related SDG indicators.

Content and Structure of This Report

This report is intended for NSOs, as well as line ministries and other relevant government units involved in the production, analysis, and communication of labor and employment data. It features challenges and solutions and highlights lessons learned and directions for future work to better produce, analyze, and communicate statistics from administrative data sources for the employment and work-related SDGs.

It complements and contributes to the increasingly available resources[2] that address the capacity-strengthening efforts in this area. These resources include the ADB handbook titled Using Administrative Data Sources for Compiling Millennium Development Goals and Related Indicators (ADB 2010) and related indicators and outcomes of the expert clinics organized by the Collaborative on Use of Administrative Data for Statistics and Global Partnership for Sustainable Development Data (GPSDD).

In addition to data and information compiled from conducting desk research, the discussion presented in this report also benefits from results of the SUADCEI as well as case studies based on interviews of NSOs and labor ministries in selected economies in Asia and the Pacific. Discussions are also supplemented by the documented wealth of experiences in other regions of the world.

Part A gives an overview of the rationale and objectives of this report and the status of use of administrative data in Asia and the Pacific. It discusses the policy context and the logical linkages between targets, policy outcomes, and monitoring indicators. It then focuses on a discussion of why and how administrative data as input data should be increasingly considered by national statistical systems for producing these estimates. The objectives of this report and its content and structure are presented to guide users on how to optimize its use.

---

[2]   See, for example, the inventory listing at United Nations Statistics Division and Global Partnership for Sustainable Development Data. Collaborative on the Use of Administrative Data for Statistics. https://unstats.un.org/capacity-development/admin-data/Inventory.

Part B introduces organizing frameworks of labor statistics and takes a close look at the SDGs and its work and employment-related goal, targets, and indicators. It includes an overview of the various sources of the input data for producing the indicator estimates and specifics for the decent work indicators in the SDG monitoring framework. It highlights the major challenges in increasing the effective use of administrative data and a broad road map for applying solutions to these challenges.

Part C highlights examples of what economies have been able to accomplish by using administrative data. Given the broad road map described in part B, part C discusses capacity building needs of national statistical systems to make use of administrative data for work and employment-related indicators for monitoring the SDGs.

Using Administrative Data for Producing Sustainable Development Goals Work and Labor-Related Monitoring Indicators: The Landscape

III. Overview of Labor Statistics and Related Sustainable Development Goal Indicators

Framework of Labor Statistics

Box 4: What Are Labor Statistics?

Labor statistics are a body of official statistics that deals with work, productive activities, workers, the characteristics of the labor market and the way it operates. They encompass a wide range of topics and link to many other bodies of official statistics, such as economic, education, and health statistics, to name a few.

Labor statistics refer to the productive activities of workers, and the labor market deficiencies associated with them. Work comprises any activity performed by persons of any sex and age to produce goods or to provide services for use by others or for own use, and labor statistics potentially cover all forms of work. This includes work for pay or profit for use by others (employment), work not for pay or profit for use by others (unpaid trainee work, volunteer work, and other work activities) and work for own final use (own-use production work).

Labor statistics refer both to labor demand and supply. Statistics about labor demand include data on the number and characteristics of enterprises, jobs, and vacancies as well as the costs of hiring. Statistics about labor supply deal with the working-age population, presenting data on its size, structure, and characteristics, and more specifically, information on employment, unemployment, and persons outside the labor force. Some of the main characteristics of jobs and employment covered by labor statistics include earnings, working time, economic activity, occupation, status in employment, establishment size, sector (private or public sector and formal or informal sector), social dialogue, occupational injuries, and social security coverage.

Source: International Labour Organization. 2017. *Quick Guide on Sources and Uses of Labour Statistics.* Geneva.

The first chart in Figure 3 lays out the framework for distinguishing the different forms of work described in Box 4. The chart below presents the same items with a representation of "paid" and "unpaid" work. This distinction is useful in particular in defining indicator SDG 5.4.1 (proportion of time spent on unpaid domestic and care work, by sex, age, and location).

Figure 4 summarizes the items within the scope of labor statistics described in Box 4. When looking at work from employment, some of the basic indicators that are produced are shown in Table 4.

Figure 3: Forms of Work Framework

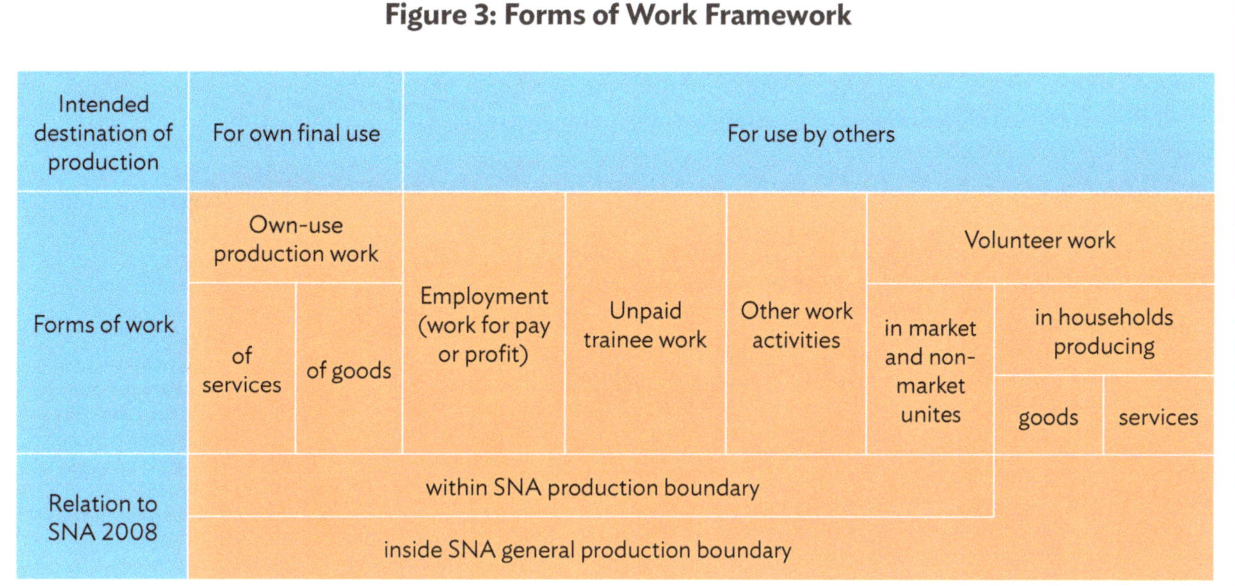

SNA = System of National Accounts.
Source: International Labour Organization. 2022. *Quick guide to understanding the impact of the new statistical standards on ILOSTAT databases*. Geneva.

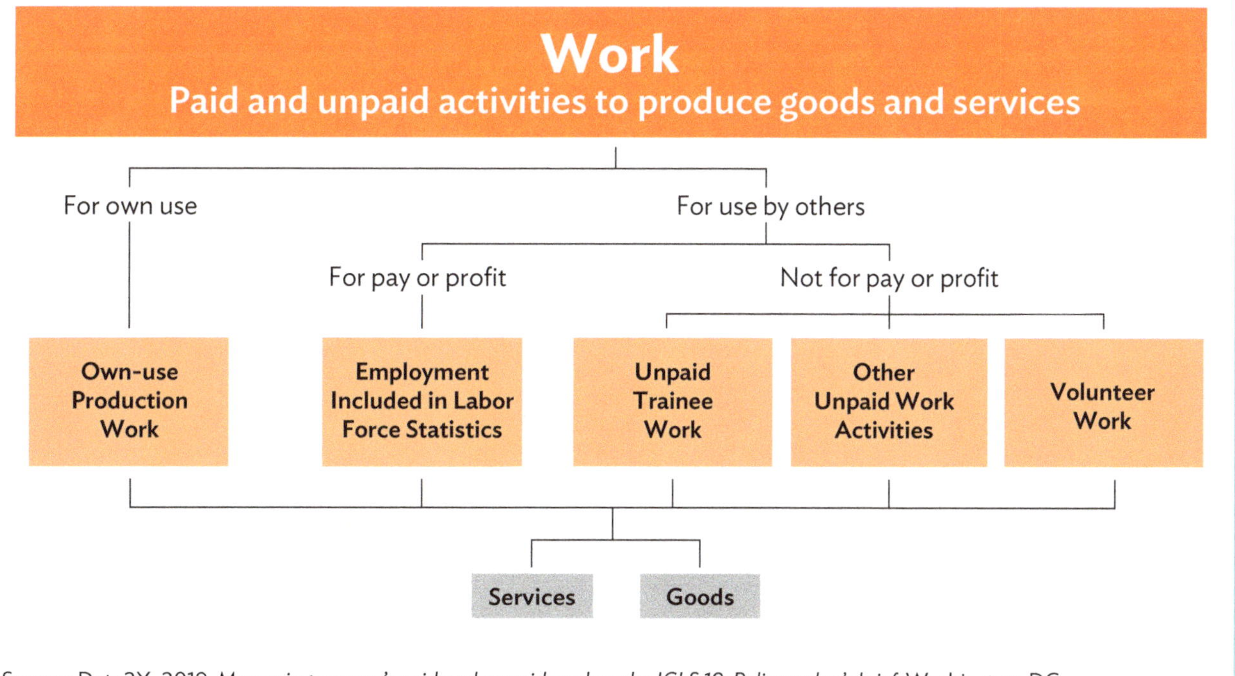

Source: Data2X. 2019. *Measuring women's paid and unpaid work under ICLS 19: Policymaker's brief*. Washington, DC.

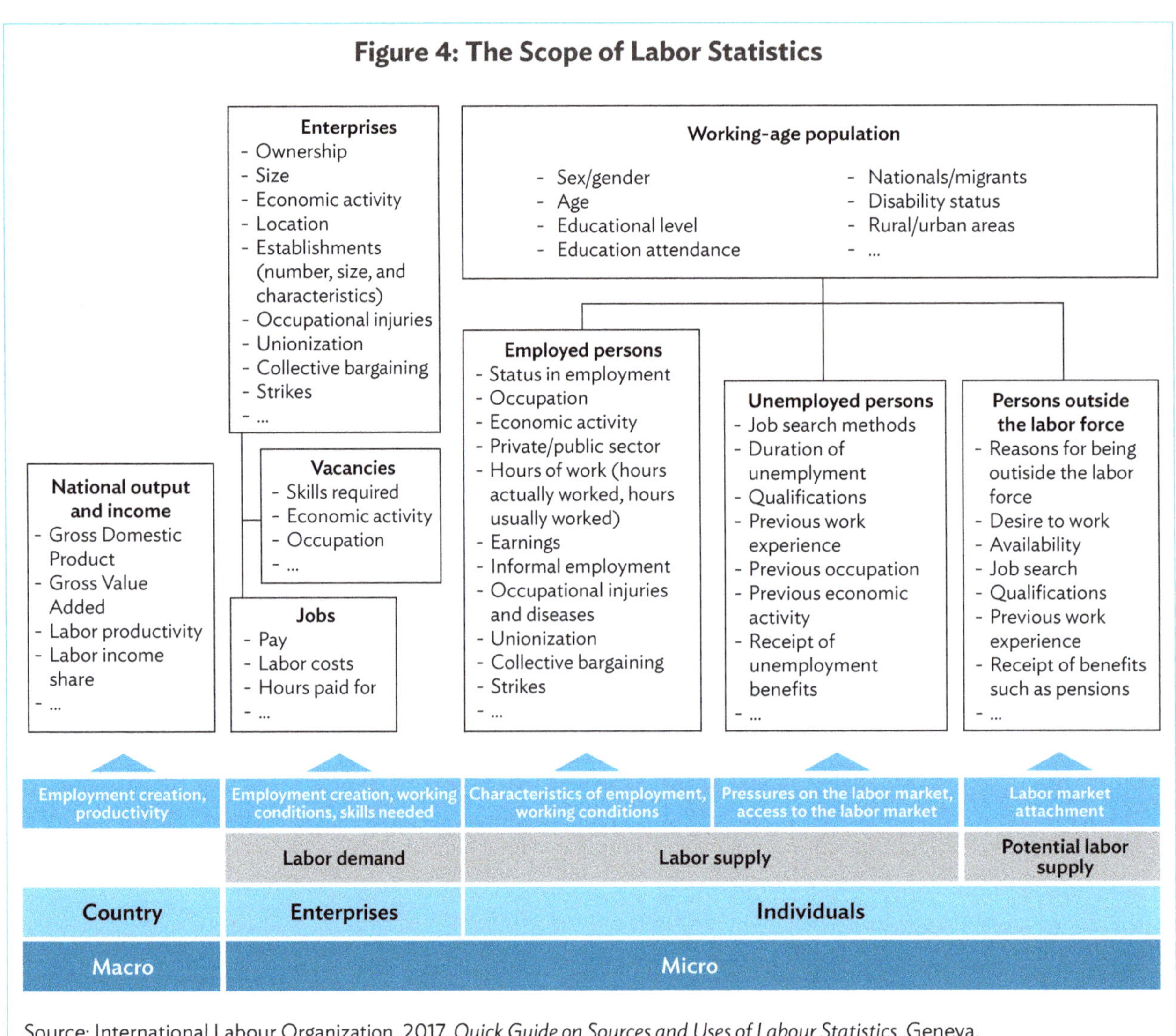

Figure 4: The Scope of Labor Statistics

Source: International Labour Organization. 2017. *Quick Guide on Sources and Uses of Labour Statistics*. Geneva.

Table 4: Key Indicators of Work from Employment

Population	Employment	Dimensions
Labor force participation rate	Employment-to-population ratio	Sex
Persons outside the labor force	Status in employment	Age
	Employment by sector	Educational attainment
	Employment by occupation	Literacy
	Employment in the informal economy	Poverty (working poor)
	Hours of work	Income distribution
	Part-time workers	Labor productivity
	Wages and compensation costs	
	Unemployment	
	Youth unemployment	
	Long-term unemployment	
	Time-related underemployment	

Source: Authors' compilation.

Sustainable Development Goal Targets and Indicators for Decent Work Outcomes

The decent work agenda is enshrined in SDG 8 (promote sustained, inclusive and sustainable economic growth, full and productive employment and decent work for all) but also cuts across seven other SDGs: SDG 1 (end poverty), SDG 4 (ensure quality education), SDG 5 (achieve gender equality), SDG 10 (reduce inequality), SDG 14 (conserve marine resources), and SDG 16 (promote justice and institutions). Table 5 summarizes the targets and indicators that are the focus of this report.

Table 5: Sustainable Development Goal Decent Work Targets and Related Indicators

Target Number	Target	Indicator Number	Indicator
1.1	By 2030, eradicate extreme poverty for all people everywhere, currently measured as people living on less than $1.25 a day	1.1.1	Proportion of population below the international poverty line, by sex, age, employment status, and geographic location (urban or rural)
1.3	Implement nationally appropriate social protection systems and measures for all, including floors, and by 2030 achieve substantial coverage of the poor and the vulnerable	1.3.1	Proportion of population covered by social protection floors or systems, by sex, distinguishing children, unemployed persons, older persons, persons with disabilities, pregnant women, newborns, work-injury victims, and the poor and the vulnerable
1.a	Ensure significant mobilization of resources from a variety of sources, including through enhanced development cooperation, in order to provide adequate and predictable means for developing countries, in particular least developed countries, to implement programs and policies to end poverty in all its dimensions	1.a.2	Proportion of total government spending on essential services (education, health, and social protection)
4.3	By 2030, ensure equal access for all women and men to affordable and quality technical, vocational and tertiary education, including university	4.3.1	Participation rate of youth and adults in formal and nonformal education and training in the previous 12 months, by sex
5.5	Ensure women's full and effective participation and equal opportunities for leadership at all levels of decision-making in political, economic and public life	5.5.2	Proportion of women in managerial positions
8.2	Achieve higher levels of economic productivity through diversification, technological upgrading, and innovation, including through a focus on high-value added and labor-intensive sectors	8.2.1	Annual growth rate of real gross domestic product per employed person

continued on next page

Table 5 *continued*

Target Number	Target	Indicator Number	Indicator
8.3	Promote development-oriented policies that: (i) support productive activities, decent job creation, entrepreneurship, creativity, and innovation; and (ii) encourage the formalization and growth of micro-, small- and medium-sized enterprises, including through access to financial services	8.3.1	Proportion of informal employment in nonagricultural employment, by sex
8.5	By 2030, achieve full and productive employment and decent work for all women and men, including for young people and persons with disabilities, and equal pay for work of equal value	8.5.1	Average hourly earnings of female and male employees, by occupation, age, and persons with disabilities
		8.5.2	Unemployment rate, by sex, age, and persons with disabilities
8.6	By 2020, substantially reduce the proportion of youth not in employment, education, or training	8.6.1	Proportion of youth (aged 15–24 years) not in education, employment, or training
8.7	Take immediate and effective measures to eradicate forced labor, end modern slavery and human trafficking and secure the prohibition and elimination of the worst forms of child labor, including recruitment and use of child soldiers, and by 2025 end child labor in all its forms	8.7.1	Proportion and number of children aged 5–17 years engaged in child labor, by sex and age
8.8	Protect labor rights and promote safe and secure working environments for all workers, including migrant workers, in particular women migrants, and those in precarious employment	8.8.1	Frequency rates of fatal and nonfatal occupational injuries, by sex and migrant status
		8.8.2	Level of national compliance with labor rights (freedom of association and collective bargaining) based on International Labour Organization textual sources and national legislation, by sex and migrant status
8.b	By 2020, develop and operationalize a global strategy for youth employment and implement the Global Jobs Pact of the International Labour Organization	8.b.1	Existence of a developed and operationalized national strategy for youth employment, as a distinct strategy or as part of a national employment strategy
10.4	Adopt policies, especially fiscal, wage and social protection policies, and progressively achieve greater equality	10.4.1	Labor's share of gross domestic product, comprising wages and social protection transfers
10.7	Facilitate orderly, safe, regular and responsible migration and mobility of people, including through the implementation of planned and well-managed migration policies	10.7.1	Recruitment cost borne by employee as a proportion of monthly income earned in country of destination

continued on next page

Table 5 *continued*

Target Number	Target	Indicator Number	Indicator
14.c	Enhance the conservation and sustainable use of oceans and their resources by implementing international law as reflected in the United Nations Convention on the Law of the Sea, which provides the legal framework for the conservation and sustainable use of oceans and their resources, as recalled in paragraph 158 of "The future we want"	14.c.1	Number of countries making progress in ratifying, accepting and implementing through legal, policy and institutional frameworks, ocean-related instruments that implement international law, as reflected in the United Nations Convention on the Law of the Sea, for the conservation and sustainable use of the oceans and their resources
16.7	Ensure responsive, inclusive, participatory, and representative decision-making at all levels	16.7.1	Proportions of positions in national and local institutions, including (i) the legislatures, (ii) the public service, and (iii) the judiciary compared to national distributions, by sex, age, persons with disabilities, and population groups
16.10	Ensure public access to information and protect fundamental freedoms, in accordance with national legislation and international agreements	16.10.1	Number of verified cases of killing, kidnapping, enforced disappearance, arbitrary detention, and torture of journalists, associated media personnel, trade unionists, and human rights advocates in the previous 12 months

Sources: United Nations Statistics Division. SDG Indicators: Metadata repository (accessed 14 December 2022); and United Nations Statistics Division. Mapping of SDG Indicators (accessed 24 August 2023).

IV. Data Sources for Work and Labor Market Indicators: Focus on Administrative Data

Overview of Data Sources for Labor Statistics

Input data sources for statistics and indicators can be divided into three groups: (i) census and survey data, (ii) big data, and (iii) administrative data.

(i)　Census and Survey Data

    (a)　How censuses and surveys are being used to provide employment- and work- related data and statistics

        In the context of compiling data and statistics for an economy's labor market information system, a labor force survey (LFS) is considered one of the main sources of comprehensive and consistent data on employment, unemployment, and persons outside the labor force. The LFS provides comprehensive source of information on all aspects of the labor market, covering the whole population, in which each person aged 15 and older can be assigned a labor force status (employed, unemployed, or outside the labor force). Since a survey covers all members in the sampled households, household surveys provide a consistent framework, with relevant disaggregation, to simultaneously study employment, unemployment, and persons outside the labor force. The unemployment rate and other indicators of the labor market are typically sourced from the LFS.

        Labor and employment data, such as income, working time, and employees, can also be collected through censuses and/or sample surveys of establishments. In general, surveys of establishments are less expensive and more cost-effective than surveys of households. Establishment censuses, by their very nature of covering all businesses, are more costly and are conducted less frequently than sample surveys of establishments. Further, establishment inquiries do not cover the self-employed (employers, own-account workers, and contributing family workers, among others) and gig workers (those who work temporary jobs in single projects or tasks typically in the service sector through digital labor platforms). They also rarely cover informal sector establishments, even if these represent a notable share of the labor market.

    (b)　Census and survey data as compared with administrative data

Table 6 summarizes and compares key features of censuses, surveys, and administrative data.

Table 6: Comparison of Censuses, Surveys, and Administrative Records as Sources of Statistical Data

Features	Censuses	Surveys	Administrative Data
1. Coverage	Complete coverage of the population is the objective	May have under coverage problems if the population frame chosen for sampling is not apt	Administrative requirements define the target populations
2. Content	Allows extensive cross-classification because of the large number of potential classification variables	The range of topics is usually covered in more depth however, than in censuses	Limited to variables needed for administrative purposes; may be subject to discontinuities
3. Concepts and definitions	Defined by statistical and analytical requirements	Defined by statistical and analytical requirements	Defined by administrative requirements
4. Small area estimates	Available because of the aim of complete coverage	Unavailable in most cases	Available, depending on the administrative process and its coverage of geographical areas and subpopulations.
5. Quality control	Can be designed to minimize errors	Since smaller in size, it allows for even tighter control than in censuses	Quality control is managed by the administrative agency; may not get needed attention except for key variables
6. Cost	Costly	Cost per survey is relatively low but cumulative cost over time may be high	Relatively inexpensive if the initial collection costs are attributed to the administrative program
7. Frequency	Usually conducted every 5 or 10 years	Usually annual, quarterly, or monthly	Usually annual or monthly depending on the administrative program
8. Timeliness	Data usually becomes available from 6 months to 2.5 years after data collection	Data from repeated regular surveys are usually available in a few weeks; ad hoc surveys may take longer	Dependent on the administrative process
9. Stability	Changes are under the control of statisticians	Changes are infrequent in the case of repeated surveys	Changes in legislation, regulation or administrative practice may cause changes
10. Respondent burden	Not frequent, but heavy	Relatively light	No additional burden

Source: Authors' compilation.

(ii)   Big Data

Big data is another potentially useful source of data for development. Although there is no standard definition of big data, it can be viewed as digital fingerprints that are unfiltered by-products or exhaust from the use of information and communication technology tools. These digital tools include electronic devices (smartphones, tablets, laptops); social media; blogs; search engines; and (fixed and mobile) sensors and tracking devices (including climate sensors and global positioning system). Big data is characterized by four Vs: (i) volume (i.e., the amount of data); (ii) velocity (i.e., the speed of data); (iii) variety (i.e., the range of data formats including personal documents, SMS messages, photos, videos, maps, and financial or social transactions); and (iv) veracity (trustworthiness of the data). While access to and storage of a large volume of data for analytics have existed in business for quite a while, the use of big data for development only gained traction in recent years with the recognition that this non-traditional data source can fill in the data gaps for monitoring the SDGs (Martinez et al. 2018; Albert and Martinez 2018; Albert et al. 2019).

A large portion of big data are geospatial data (Lee and Kang 2015). Geospatial data are time-based data that are associated with specific location on the Earth's surface. They are large datasets that are processed using nontraditional GIS tools. The use of geospatial information offers several benefits. Among others, it can help improve decision-making with use of simplified data, improved communication plan (especially during crisis), more effective planning methods for risk-based scenarios, developments, or community changes, and optimized business processes (Mirdamadi 2022).

Online job portals are a common source of big data. They have unique qualities that can provide real-time information; rich, granular text information about skill demand and supply; information about actual labor market transactions and the job matching process, and information that link employers and jobseekers. Hayashi et al. (2022) demonstrated how online job portals can provide a quick perspective on the labor demand in post pandemic labor markets. In Pakistan, an online job portal (Rozee.pk), was developed to provide information on labor market conditions as well as skill demand and supply in Pakistan. The Government of India launched the National Career Service through the country's Ministry of Labour and Employment in 2015. It is India's largest employment platform, and it aims to attract about 20 million job seekers and 900,000 establishments and companies. This platform also publishes data on vacancies and the number of employers registered.

In Southeast Asia, the Employment and Skills Strategies in Southeast Asia initiative helps the exchange of experiences on employment and skills development (Martinez-Fernandez and Powell 2010). Primarily, it aims to guide policymakers on what policy approaches to take to tackle various cross-cutting labor market issues, build the capacity of practitioners in implementing effective local employment and skills development strategies, and assist in the development of governance mechanisms conducive to policy integration and partnership at the local level.

(iii)   Administrative Data

Collections of data on persons and firms held usually by government agencies are collected and used for the purposes of administering taxes, benefits, or services. Data collected on pensions, taxation, social protection records, registered unemployment, and occupational injuries are examples of administrative data. Though administrative data are effective in complementing survey data, these data are especially useful in economies where household or establishment surveys are hardly conducted, thus serving a purpose as an alternative data source for statistical compilation. Since 2016, Australia has used administrative data to develop an address register, which significantly helped reduce the cost of conducting its census by mailing out access codes and forms online to Australians instead of delivering them in person. Nordic countries such as Denmark, Finland, Norway, and Sweden have established their population registers as early as the 1960s and used them in their census starting in the 70s (UNECE 2007).

Administrative data can be used to produce statistics in a cost-effective way compared to designing a specialized data collection activity solely intended to serve specific data needs. With administrative data, a complete count of units can be produced as in censuses (assuming full coverage of the population of interest). So, just like censuses, administrative data can yield disaggregated data for subpopulations, even rare ones.

The complete coverage in administrative systems is a huge advantage, as it contains records on persons who may not be willing to participate in surveys. Statistics from administrative data can also be more accurate than survey-based statistics because some measurement issues (e.g., forgetting, social-desirability bias) are avoided. Further, since administrative data systems can provide detailed longitudinal information (e.g., income, medical expenditure), this can potentially provide an examination of living standards over time. On the other hand, such information may be too burdensome for respondents to report in surveys.

(a)   The use of administrative records to produce work and employment-related statistics has several advantages.

Firstly, administrative data usually constitute a full count of all "clients" of the underlying administrative system, such as social protection beneficiaries or unemployed registrants, so a complete count of the clients in the system can be done with all the records of the system available for use in the statistical compilation. Administrative sources thus quite often give complete, or almost complete, coverage of their target population(s). As a result, statistics can be produced at rather granular levels, i.e., small areas (districts, towns, and provinces) and rare groups (persons with disability), without concern for issues of precision as in sample surveys.

Secondly, since the data on the clients in an administrative system have already been collected as part of an administrative function, the records created and maintained by the administrative data owner agency are readily available. There are few costs and coordination mechanisms are less complicated in accessing the administrative records and deriving statistics from the records for statistical purposes. Further, there are no additional response burdens: the data that the units of inquiry have already provided as part of an administrative process (registration, application, inspection, notification) may be used for the statistical compilation without the clients of the administrative system having to be involved in a separate statistical inquiry on the same or related topics. This is also a strong motive to use administrative data, especially if the clients of the administrative system are businesses. While businesses typically understand the reasons for supplying data for registration and tax purposes, they are likely to consider statistical inquiries (i.e., surveys and censuses) as burdensome.

Finally—related to the reductions in cost and response burden in administrative systems—administrative data may allow statistics to be produced more frequently, and thus generate timely statistical outputs, particularly when the administrative data source is updated frequently.

(b)   On their own, none of these data sources can meet all data user needs; at best, they complement each other in contributing to enhanced compilation of development statistics.

(c)   In the context of SDG 8, all these data sources also contribute to an economy's labor market information system. By recognizing the strengths, limitations and complementarities of the various types of data sources available, the knowledge gained about the labor market gets wider from the spectrum of available work and employment-related statistics. The features of the data source ultimately determine the quality of labor statistics and labor indicators; thus, it is crucial to understand the data source used—considering the methodology and coverage of the underlying data source.

Different data sources for labor and employment statistics can enrich each other. Census data on population and on establishment can be used for benchmarking and to develop sample frames for sample surveys of households and establishments, as well as population or business registers. Data from sample surveys provide intercensal estimates and be used to monitor short-term trends. Administrative data can complement data from censuses and sample surveys, and at the same time, survey and census data can help in offsetting under-registration in administrative records. To fully leverage the available data sources, coherence must be ensured among the data sources in terms of statistical methodological guidelines used (e.g., concepts, definitions, classifications, reference periods.).

Data Sources for Producing Sustainable Development Goal Decent Work Indicators

Table 7 provides information on existing data sources utilized by economies in compiling the decent work-related SDG indicators.

Table 7: Sustainable Development Goal Employment and Related Indicators and Data Sources

SDG Indicator Number	SDG Indicator Title	Data Source(s)
1.1.1	Proportion of population below the international poverty line, by sex, age, employment status and geographical location (urban or rural)	Household surveys (household income and expenditure survey, household budget survey, LSMS with employment modules, or LFS with information on household income)
1.3.1	Proportion of population covered by social protection floors/systems, by sex, distinguishing children, unemployed persons, older persons, persons with disabilities, pregnant women, newborns, work injury victims and the poor and the vulnerable	Administrative data, household surveys (partially)

continued on next page

Table 7 *continued*

SDG Indicator Number	SDG Indicator Title	Data Source(s)
1.a.2	Proportion of total government spending on essential services (education, health and social protection)	Annual financial reports by national ministries of finance or ministries of education, or national accounts reports by national statistics offices, government expenditure datasets, expenditure reports in national and sub-national budgets, the IMF Government Finance Statistics database, public expenditure reviews published by the World Bank and others, the World Bank's BOOST dataset
4.3.1	Participation rate of youth and adults in formal and non-formal education and training in the previous 12 months, by sex	Household surveys (LFS or LSMS)
5.5.2	Proportion of women in managerial positions	Household surveys (LFS or other types of household surveys with module on employment), administrative data (alternative)
8.2.1	Annual growth rate of real gross domestic product per employed person	Household surveys (LFS) or other survey with information on the working activities of the working-age population
8.3.1	Proportion of informal employment in nonagricultural employment, by sex	Household surveys (LFS or LSMS) and mixed surveys as identified in the ILO Manual
8.5.1	Average hourly earnings of female and male employees, by occupation, age, and persons with disabilities	Household surveys; establishment surveys
8.5.2	Unemployment rate, by sex, age, and persons with disabilities	Household surveys (LFS, LSMS, or other household survey with information on employment and unemployment)
8.6.1	Proportion of youth (aged 15–24 years) not in education, employment, or training	Household surveys (LFS, LSMS, or other household survey with information on employment and unemployment)
8.7.1	Proportion and number of children aged 5–17 years engaged in child labor, by sex and age	Household surveys (MICS, DHS, child labor surveys, LFS, or LSMS)
8.8.1	Frequency rates of fatal and non-fatal occupational injuries, by sex and migrant status	Administrative data; household surveys covering informal sector enterprises and establishment surveys (partially)
8.8.2	Level of national compliance with labor rights (freedom of association and collective bargaining) based ILO textual sources and national legislation, by sex and migrant status	ILO textual sources
8.b.1	Existence of a developed and operationalized national strategy for youth employment, as a distinct strategy or as part of a national employment strategy	Global survey for data collection
10.4.1	Labor's share of gross domestic product, comprising wages and social protection transfers	National accounts
10.7.1	Recruitment cost borne by employee as a proportion of monthly income earned in country of destination	Household surveys

continued on next page

Table 7 *continued*

SDG Indicator Number	SDG Indicator Title	Data Source(s)
14.c.1	Number of countries making progress in ratifying, accepting and implementing through legal, policy, and institutional frameworks, ocean-related instruments that implement international law, as reflected in the United Nations Convention on the Law of the Sea, for the conservation and sustainable use of the oceans and their resources	Questionnaire distributed to relevant government ministries, departments, and agencies (UNSD 2021)
16.7.1	Proportions of positions in national and local institutions, including (i) the legislatures; (ii) the public service; and (iii) the judiciary, compared to national distributions, by sex, age, persons with disabilities, and population groups	Administrative data, surveys
16.10.1	Number of verified cases of killing, kidnapping, enforced disappearance, arbitrary detention and torture of journalists, associated media personnel, trade unionists, and human rights advocates in the previous 12 months	Administrative data

DHS = demographic and health survey, ILO = International Labour Organization, IMF = International Monetary Fund, LFS = labor force survey, LSMS = living standards measurement survey, MICS = multiple indicator cluster survey, UNSD = United Nations Statistics Division.

Sources: UNSD. SDG Indicators: Metadata repository (accessed 14 December 2022); and UNSD. Mapping of SDG Indicators (accessed 24 August 2023).

V. Issues and Challenges and the Potential Solutions in Using Administrative Data

Issues and Challenges

The use of data from administrative data systems or records for producing official statistics presents many challenges— a major reason being that the data collected are not originally designed for statistical purposes. The main issues and challenges based on the SUADCEI responses from NSOs and labor and social ministries are displayed in Figure 5. For the NSOs and labor and social welfare ministries that responded in the survey, data quality concerns stood out among the challenges they encountered.

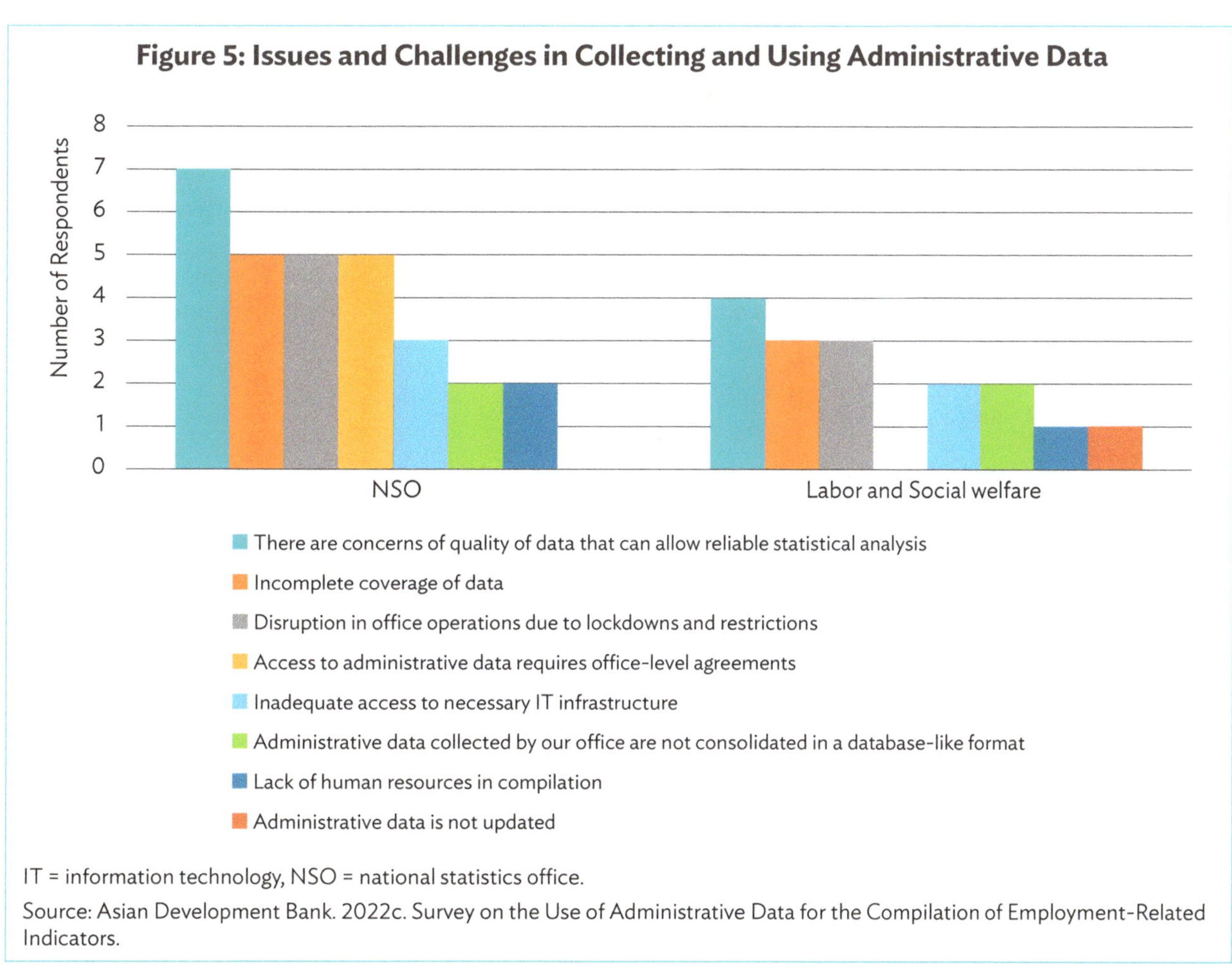

Figure 5: Issues and Challenges in Collecting and Using Administrative Data

IT = information technology, NSO = national statistics office.

Source: Asian Development Bank. 2022c. Survey on the Use of Administrative Data for the Compilation of Employment-Related Indicators.

Some specific issues are illustrated as follows:

(i)   Technical Aspects

(a)   Units of Observation

As pointed out in ILO/East Asia Multidisciplinary Advisory Team (1997), the units used in some administrative records may not satisfy the statistical needs of data users (e.g., establishments versus enterprises or jobs versus persons). A definition of the unit in an administrative system may also be incompatible with other data sources. Some data systems register persons or businesses, while others register events. For instance, occupational injuries from insurance records pertain to cases of injuries. Consequently, the statistics generated would refer to the number of injuries incurred, and not the number of injuries incurred by different people (as one worker may have more than one occupational injury), but there may be no way to account for this unless the records on injuries have the names of the persons injured.

(b)   Content, Scope, and Coverage

The data content may be constrained by law or some other reason. Coding of important data may also be constrained. The metadata, i.e., descriptions and background for coding, may be incomplete or limited.

Some administrative data systems may have too narrow a scope (certain categories of units are excluded by design), while others may have too broad a scope (they may include groups). At job fairs, for instance, the "registered jobseekers" category might include those employed who are seeking additional jobs or a change of jobs and exclude those unemployed who have not registered.

The data collection forms used in administrative data systems may exclude information of relevance, for example, education, household composition, self-employment income, habits and behaviors, opinions, and retirement plans.

(c)   Data Quality and Updating

Maintenance procedures of administrative data systems may not provide the data quality needed for official statistics. For example, procedures may not require the removal of expired records, or the updating of details after a person is first registered. There may be erroneous data, missing data items, or missing records. Variables may also change over time without notice and without any transformation, as in the case of occupation or industry codes. Administrative procedures and the data flow through a system may also lead to delays in updating the administrative system's database. Editing the data to curate inconsistencies found and deciding on what imputation methods to use for treating missing data may be needed at times to ensure data quality.

As there can be serious data quality issues in the use of administrative records, initiatives to improve the quality of administrative data can bring about tremendous benefits for data producers and users. Administrative data are produced not just by national statistical offices (NSOs), but many government line ministries as well. It may even be likely that government line ministries are producing more administrative data than the NSOs. The large amount of data produced by government agencies as well as the private sector that could potentially supplement data gaps further emphasizes the need to ensure the quality of administrative data.

(d)   Consistency with National Statistical Definitions, Standards, and Classifications

Data from administrative records often have to be aligned with existing statistical standards and classifications before they can be utilized to produce official statistics. This would involve examining definitions, concepts and classifications used, and coding variables and deriving new ones.

Differences in statistics from administrative sources with corresponding statistics produced from other data sources arise largely from differences in variables, in coverage, in precision, in time period(s), and that result from measurement errors. Consider, for instance, unemployment registered in administrative systems versus unemployment in the LFS. Unemployed persons in an unemployment registry want to find a job and benefit from public support but some of them may actually have part time jobs. Further, not everyone who is unemployed may register, as some may seek employment instead in the informal sector. On the other hand, survey estimates of unemployment from the LFS are based on a three-criteria definition: persons (i) not employed, (ii) available for work, and (iii) looking for work. Thus, we would expect a wide difference in statistics on registered unemployment from unemployment statistics based on the LFS, as in the case of Mongolia (Box 1). See also ILO (n.d.).

Another example: registered unemployment may also be bigger than unemployment in the LFS, which means that persons registered as unemployed may not be actively seeking employment or available for employment (or even not strictly jobless, which per the unemployment definition in the LFS usually corresponds to not having worked for even 1 hour during a short reference period). Differences in unemployment and in other similar cases can be examined, with the results of the examination harmonized by appropriate action.

(ii)   Legal and Institutional Aspects

(a)   Data Sharing, Confidentiality, and Privacy Protection

The level of stringency of data sharing and data privacy-related stipulations in statistical laws or acts may create barriers and bottlenecks in promoting wider use of administrative data for statistical purposes. It is given that there needs to be a legal basis for data sharing. However, there is a need to find an optimal balance between stringency of protocols for data sharing between the NSOs and other owners of administrative data, which can ensure data privacy and confidentiality are protected, especially when data from different sources are linked and there may not have been an anticipation of the use of these data for purposes other than the administrative function of the data owner. Protocols must be in place to ensure data privacy will not be infringed when producing statistics using administrative data. In some economies, a statistics act is enforced to serve as a guide in the access and use of administrative data while data sharing arrangements among government agencies, including nonstatistical agencies, can also govern such purpose. For example, the Statistics Act of Tonga (2016 Revised Edition) mandates any ministry, department, branch, bureau, agency, or division of the Government of Tonga to provide administrative records for statistical use upon the request of the government statistician. When providing access to administrative data, the ministry, department, branch, bureau, agency, or division concerned shall set the conditions regarding storage, access, destruction, and return of records. The Statistics Act of the Republic of Korea (2007) stipulates that "the administrative data provided by public institutions shall not be used for any purpose other than the production of statistics, nor shall it be provided to other persons."

(b)   Accessibility, Coordination, and Collaboration

In addition to a legal basis for data sharing, it is important to have coordination mechanisms that foster exchange of data and metadata between the NSO and administrative data owners. A memorandum of understanding between the NSO and line ministries or other administrative data owners on a data sharing arrangement can provide a useful catalyst for increased usage of administrative data for development and policymaking. In these cases, as a trade-off for the NSO being given access to the administrative data to produce statistics from the system, the NSO could give back to the institution a quality assessment of the data or capacity building activities.

In accessing the data, some conditions need to be met to ensure data privacy and other legal provisions. For example, in some cases, data is made accessible from a secure setting where the data use is controlled and monitored, and where outputs are checked to ensure that respondents in the data system cannot be identified, that personal data cannot be disclosed, and that those with access to the microdata are accountable for data breaches.

(c)   Capacity and Associated Costs

Many developed economies have been using administrative data for statistical purposes. This is made possible through strong statistical capacities and a dynamic data ecosystem where owners of administrative data make conscious efforts to protect administrative data privacy while promoting its accessibility and use. In contrast, in economies with lower statistical capacities, there is a huge cost to cleaning and curating data from administrative sources, assuming access is given.

Statistical compilations from administrative records will usually need data processing and analytics as well as quality assessment. Key items involved include a unique identification or reference number for each record; date(s) of an event, a registration, and/or a similar occurrence; variables for classification of records in tables or graphs, e.g., sex, age, occupation; and quantitative data (e.g., income, age, weeks of employment) that should be aggregated or averaged.

Capacities are needed to simplify details for ease of interpretation, check records for completeness and accuracy, summarize data into tables and visualizations, and report and communicate results. Likewise, application of techniques such as data integration that enhance the usefulness of administrative data requires capacity building.

Strategic Actions for Enhanced Access, Use, and Management of Administrative Data in Statistical Programs of a National Statistics Office

Given the issues and challenges in the use of administrative data outlined in section V-A, NSOs can benefit from implementing a strategy for addressing these. The primary objective is for NSOs to influence, have access to and make possible use of administrative data in their statistical programs to reduce response burden, lower costs, improve quality, and produce new data series for users, while maintaining public trust in accordance with the United Nations Fundamental Principles of Official Statistics.

A broad set of strategic actions can be taken toward this end and these actions are outlined as follows:

(i)   Institutional setup within the NSO, e.g., the administrative data portfolio is clearly assigned to a team in the NSO. This team will be responsible for leading the work on enhancing the access, use, and management of administrative data. Major elements of the tasks and responsibilities involve leading and coordinating actions.

(ii)   Identification, documentation, and review of legislation that may be relevant to access, use, and management of administrative data by the NSO. The review of relevant legislation would include the following:

   (a)   Statistical act or law: what is the scope of legal authority that the NSO has to access, use, manage, and protect administrative data. What are the barriers to access, use, and manage administrative data?
   (b)   What is the impact of other existing legislation on the access, use, and management of administrative data?
   (c)   How can legislation (especially the statistical act or law) be strengthened to take down barriers to favor access, enforce use, and protect data?

(iii)   Inventory of existing administrative data sources being accessed and utilized in the NSO: starting point for developing a strategy for enhancing the access, use, and management of administrative data. Inventory information should include the following:

   (a)   Information about the data provider (e.g., ministry and contact name).
   (b)   Information about the data source (e.g., name, topic, frequency of delivery, costs, record layout).
   (c)   Existence of an agreement between the NSO and the data provider.
   (d)   Existence of quality assessment made on the data.
   (e)   Identification of the custodian of the data within the NSO (e.g., division, name of employee).

(iv)   Policy and directives for use of administrative data (covering access, privacy, and security) that sets out clearly, in the NSO's own set of policies and directives, any legislative requirements and policies and directives of the central government that pertain to access, use, and management of administrative data by the NSO to ensure a common understanding of requirements and a consistent rule. These are to be shared with data providers. This could include the following:

   (a)   Policy for the use of administrative data for statistical purposes (high-level principles and requirements). See, for example, Statistics Canada's Policy on the Use of Administrative Data Obtained under the Statistics Act.
   (b)   Directives for access, use, or management of administrative data (more detailed requirements).

(v)   Mapping out strategic collaboration initiatives with data providers: fostering collaboration with data providers through strategic communication, including transparency of the use of their data by the statistical office. These initiatives may include agreements on data acquisition between the NSO and data provider. Such agreements can be formal (e.g., a memorandum of understanding) or informal communications that provide written documentation of the exchange of data between the data provider and the NSO.

(vi)   Exploration of new administrative data sources and identification of an administrative data custodian for all data sources within the NSO. The tasks would include preliminary assessment of potential administrative data source, covering information gathering about the data provider, the data product, and the potential uses.

The tasks would also cover quality assessment in the absence of data, e.g., a data provider's institutional environment and capacity to supply quality administrative data on a timely basis, ease of accessibility, coherence with existing statistical definitions, and variables.

Based on preliminary assessments, the NSO requests the information from the provider. Box 5 provides an example from Statistics Canada on how information is requested from a data provider.

(vii)   Assessment of fitness for use when the administrative data is acquired. Once an agreement is in place and data has been received (either a partial data file or full data for a trial period), fitness for use must be assessed before deciding to use the data in the NSO statistical program. Based on the assessment, the NSO can then decide whether or not to request this data on a regular basis.

(viii)   Incorporation of fit-for-use administrative data in statistical programs.

(ix)   Management of use of administrative data to ensure that the NSO is respecting policies and directives relating to administrative data as described in item (iv) in this list.

Box 5: Request for Information from Data Providers: Example from Statistics Canada

Under the authority of the Statistics Act, Statistics Canada is hereby requesting the following information, which will be used solely for statistical and research purposes and will be protected in accordance with the provisions of the Statistics Act and any other applicable law. This is a mandatory request for data.

Employment Insurance, Social Assistance, and Other Transfers

What information is being requested?	Statistics Canada holds administrative records for the Employment Insurance Statistics program from Employment and Social Development Canada (ESDC). These administrative records include record of employment, record of employment monthly increment, employment insurance status vector, and employment insurance claimant. Additional information will be extracted from ESDC's Benefits Knowledge Hub database on the applicant (marital status) and their claim (pay week, application date, and the date the claim is established).
What personal information is included in this request?	This request includes the marital status of the applicant.
What years of data will be requested?	Statistics Canada will be requesting this new information on a weekly basis beginning January 2023 and ongoing.
From whom will the information be requested?	ESDC.
Why is this information being requested?	Through the timely acquisition of new Benefits Knowledge Hub files, Statistics Canada will be able to significantly reduce the current lag (10 weeks) on its reporting of employment insurance beneficiaries using existing administrative records from ESDC. The goal is to improve the timeliness of employment insurance reporting, by reducing the delay between the reference week and the official release, closer to the Labour Force Survey reporting (delay of approximately 4 weeks). Statistics Canada may also use the information for other statistical and research purposes.
Why were these organizations selected as data providers?	The Benefits Knowledge Hub at ESDC is responsible for collecting and maintaining data related to the employment insurance files received from applicants in Canada.
When will this information be requested?	This information will be requested in January 2023 and onward.
When was this request published?	To be determined.

Source: Government of Canada, Statistics Canada. Request for information — Labour. https://www.statcan.gc.ca/en/our-data/where/admin-rfi/labour#Employment-insurance-social-assistance.

Doing, Learning, and Building Capacity in Using Administrative Data for Producing Work- and Labor-Related Sustainable Development Goal Indicators

VI. Using Administrative Data for Work- and Labor-Related Statistics and Indicators

This section highlights initiatives undertaken by economies in using administrative data sources for producing decent work and SDG-related indicators.

(a)   Data on social protection coverage of an economy's labor force and other segments of the population are typically sourced from administrative data.

In Asia and the Pacific and other parts of the world, governments expanded their social protection programs to cushion the adverse impacts of socioeconomic shocks such as high food prices, job losses, income flow disruptions, and death of household members resulting from the COVID-19 pandemic. The need for relevant and timely data to do so highlighted the importance of access to and use of administrative data.

Mongolia

Social welfare programs in Mongolia consist of cash transfers and social services designed to support poor and vulnerable groups such as older people, people with disabilities, orphans and their caretakers, pregnant mothers and mothers who have given birth to many children, and veterans with state honors. More specifically, there are 72 social welfare programs in Mongolia (ADB 2017), one of which is the Food Stamp Program (FSP) which provides cash transfers to poor people.

The FSP, implemented by the Ministry of Labor and Social Protection, was piloted in 2008 as a response to high food prices that were experienced in that year and as a means of protecting the country's most vulnerable. The FSP was made into a permanent program funded by the Government of Mongolia as a result of the 2012 Social Welfare Law. In 2018, the Ministry of Labor and Social Protection introduced several employment conditions for FSP beneficiaries.[3] This information generates data that can be used for various employment statistics. The FSP has a wealth of information in its administrative data system (Box 6).

---

[3]   For able-bodied working-age persons, the FSP requires that a person must either be employed or, if not, they must register with the employment office and engage in employment promotion activities (including employment orientation and counselling services, employment training, public works, and community works under the local governor's office). These employment conditions, however, do not apply to (i) pregnant women or postpartum mothers; (ii) a person caring for a child under 6 not enrolled in preschool education; (iii) a person taking care of another person in need of permanent care; (iv) those engaged in full-time education (university, college, or technical and vocational education); (v) anyone who has lost 70% or more of their ability to work; and (vi) herders. As of June 2021, the employment conditions were reinforced with the specification that, if an eligible household member does not register with the employment office and refuses two job offers, the food stamp benefits are terminated. Beyond these changes, the draft of the new social welfare law under preparation in 2022 is considering introducing time limits to the receipt of food stamps or reduction of the benefit amount after 2 years (to prevent welfare dependency).

Box 6: Administrative Data of Mongolia's Food Stamp Program

The information collected from the Integrated Household Database and FSP database (history of payments) for implementing the Food Stamp Program (FSP) comprise the administrative data system of the FSP. The Integrated Household Database contains information on FSP household beneficiaries from three assessments (the first conducted in 2010–2012, the second in 2013, and the third in 2017—which can be used to determine how employment conditions have changed, as well as how the living standards have changed for FSP beneficiaries. In addition, it has information on the duration of FSP support and provides some information on reasons for people's employment status and the barriers and constraints they face in obtaining and maintaining a job.

As pointed out in Asian Development Bank (2021c), these data can be linked with another administrative database, the National Insurance Database, maintained by the Social Insurance General Office (to identify the social insurance contribution history of FSP beneficiaries). Data integration of the FSP database with the Integrated Household Database, as well as with the National Insurance Database, is possible through the unique national individual identification numbers recorded in all databases. Therefore, no information is available on (i) people's skills; (ii) their experience in accessing employment services; or (iii) the factors that enable some people, but not others, to find work.

Source: Asian Development Bank. 2022b. *Mongolia: Building Capacity for an Effective Social Welfare System.* Consultant's report. Manila (TA 9893-MON). https://www.adb.org/sites/default/files/project-documents/51387/51387-001-tacr-en_1.pdf.

(b)   Administrative data provide rich information that can be used as inputs when designing social protection-related policies.

Philippines

The Philippine Statistics Authority produces statistics on the total pensioners (formerly employed in the private and public sectors) who receive retirement/old age pensions on a lifetime cash benefit paid every month as a percentage share of total household population 60 years old and over.[4] Data on this indicator is sourced from administrative data systems of the Government Service Insurance System (which provides old-age contributory pensions for formal workers in the public sector) and the Social Security System (which provides old-age contributory pensions for formal workers in the private sector). Since 2011, old age noncontributory pensions have also been provided to indigent persons 60 years and older through the Social Pension program of the Department of Social Welfare and Development (Albert et al. 2021). Figure 6 illustrates the old-age pension coverage for persons aged 60 and older in the Philippines from the three pension programs combined. Data is sourced from the administrative data systems of these pension programs.

If the age of the elderly group is restricted to those 65 years and older, then this corresponds to the sub-indicator of SDG 1.3.1 on the "proportion of population above statutory pensionable age receiving a pension" as the mandatory retirement in the Philippines is set at 65 years. Since information on the sex of individuals is included in the records of pensioners for the two contributory pension programs and the noncontributory program, the indicator can be computed with sex disaggregation as listed in the SDG Global Indicators Database and summarized in Table 8.

---

4   Philippine Statistics Authority. Metadata on Decent Work Statistics. https://openstat.psa.gov.ph/Metadata/3K3E1004 (accessed 24 August 2023).

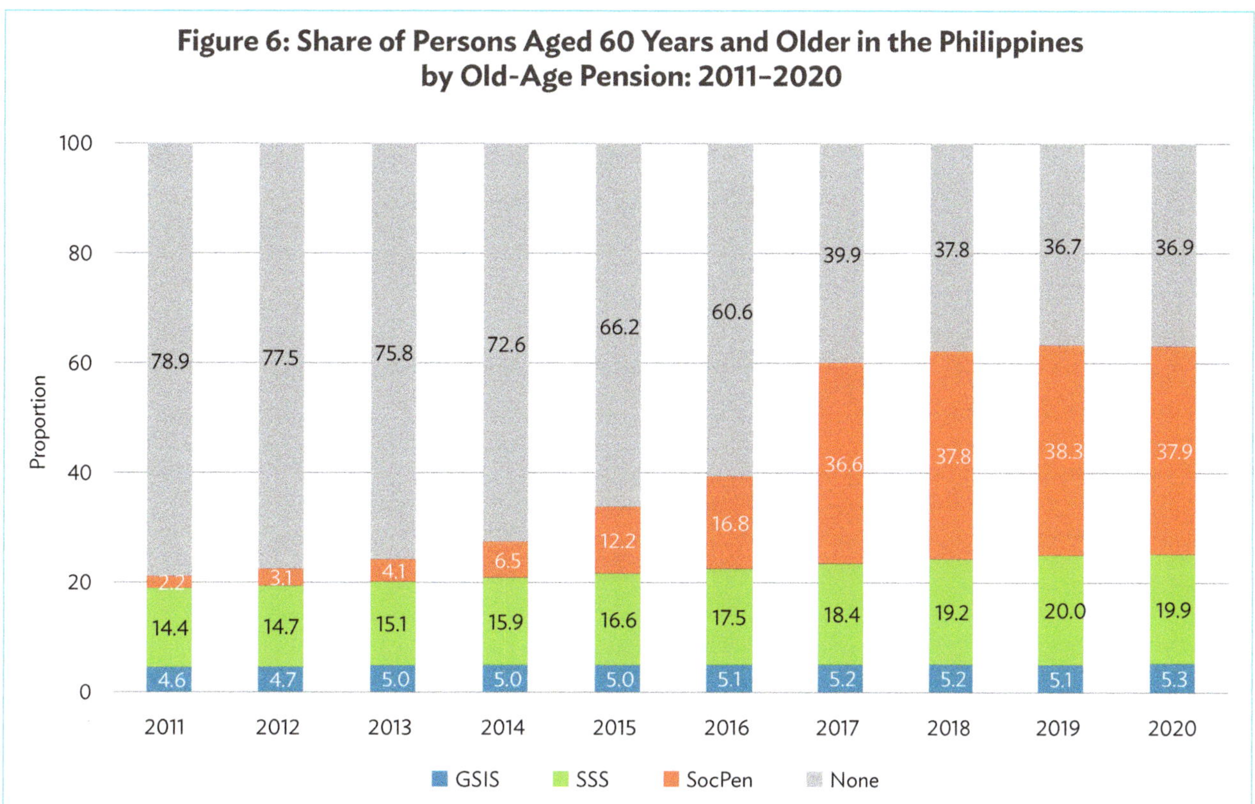

Figure 6: Share of Persons Aged 60 Years and Older in the Philippines by Old-Age Pension: 2011–2020

GSIS = Government Service Insurance System, SSS = Social Security System, SocPen = Social Pension Program.

Sources: Administrative data sourced from the SSS, GSIS, and population projections of the Philippine Statistics Authority based on Philippine Statistics Authority. 2012. 2010 Census of Population and Housing. Manila (Table 4). https://psa.gov.ph/system/files/phcd/2022-12/Table4_9.pdf.

Table 8: Proportion of Population above Statutory Pensionable Age Receiving a Pension, by Sex

Year	Value (%)	Sex
2016	39.8	Both sexes
2020	20.5	Both sexes
2020	12.0	Female
2020	23.3	Male

Source: United Nations Statistics Division. Sustainable Development Goal Indicators Database https://unstats.un.org/sdgs/dataportal/database (accessed 22 December 2022).

Singapore

Administrative records from the Central Provident Fund provide information on resident employees, defined as employees who have at least one contribution to the fund. The Central Provident Fund is a compulsory savings scheme intended to provide workers financial security in their old age, including helping meet the needs of health care, homeownership, family protection, and asset enhancement. Data on nonresidents working in Singapore can be sourced from the administrative records of the Ministry of Manpower, the government agency authorized to issue work passes for non-residents.

Singapore also has a labor market information system that provides data on employment, unemployment, income, job vacancies, retrenchment, and labor turnover drawn from administrative records and surveys on establishments, individuals, and households.

(c)   Data integration. In a number of instances, harnessing administrative data for enhanced compilation of work-related, employment-related, and other development indicators requires merging it with data from other sources.

Data integration can include any or all of the following activities (UNESCAP 2020): (i) combining data from multiple sources as part of the production of integrated statistics, such as national accounts; (ii) combining geospatial data with statistical data or other nonstatistical data; (iii) pooling data, with the aim of increasing the effective number of observations of some phenomena; (iv) matching record linkage routines, with the objective to link micro or macro data from different data sources; (v) fusing data (integration followed by reduction or replacement); and (vi) prioritizing, when two or more data sources contain information on the same variable, with potentially different values. The results of data integration are a single enlarged and/or higher quality dataset. Data integration combines the strengths in each of the data sources and mitigates their disadvantages. Further, it increases the number of relevant variables for statistical compilation and other research purposes.

Data integration has tremendous potential toward addressing data gaps such as lack of disaggregated SDG data. Results of the SUADCEI show that only 21.7% of NSOs in Asia and the Pacific reported having engaged in data integration work involving administrative data. Although only few have experienced administrative data-related initiatives, it has great potential. For instance, if various administrative data systems in all welfare programs in Mongolia were integrated with the FSP's Integrated Household Database, this could provide information on the poverty status of program beneficiaries, and consequently provide a disaggregation of social protection coverage by poverty status.

Figure 7 illustrates the basic idea behind data integration from various data sources. Box 7 provides a more detailed description of the process of linking.

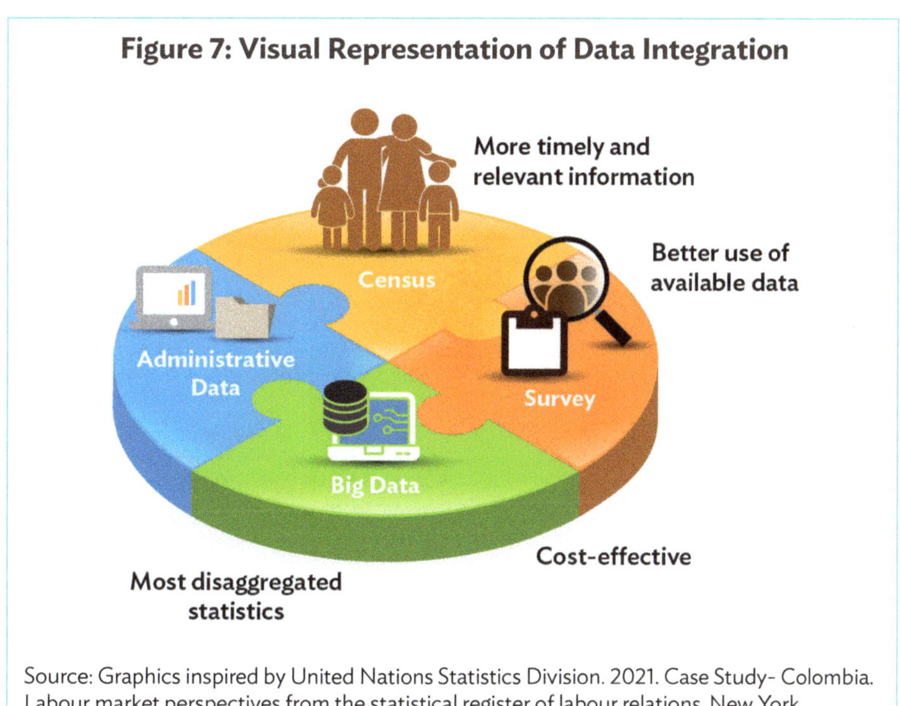

Source: Graphics inspired by United Nations Statistics Division. 2021. Case Study- Colombia. Labour market perspectives from the statistical register of labour relations. New York.

Box 7: Matching-Based Methods for Integrating Administrative Data Sources

There are various matching-based methods that can be used to integrate administrative data with other data sources. The basic idea behind data integration is linkage based on a matching variable that uniquely identifies a record in administrative data and matches this record with a corresponding survey or other administrative record(s). Different methods for linking administrative data with other data sources include exact matching and statistical matching (or data fusion). Exact matching assumes that the unique identifier is recorded without error. When data from more than one administrative data source are combined, differences in concepts, definitions, reference dates, coverage, and the data quality standards must be reconciled by applying the reconciliation at each data source. While quality is not an easily defined concept, following Brackstone (1999), the dimensions of quality in statistics involve relevance,[a] accuracy,[b] timeliness,[c] accessibility,[d] interpretability,[e] and coherence.[f] Exact matching of persons is facilitated with a record of national identification, and in its absence, the full name of a person and, if this is not enough, the address. Thus, informed consent is needed for the record linkage. Some administrative data are longitudinal (e.g., tax data) and, in this case, when records from different reference periods are linked, they can provide rich insights for researchers on dynamics; however, their use can raise serious privacy concerns.

Statistics New Zealand offers on its webpage guidance on data integration projects and privacy impact assessments. Use the identifier variable with care, as a unit may change identifiers over time. In some instances, the same unit may actually have more than one identifier for the same reference period. If this happens, there should be a mechanism for handling data duplicates. The data integration process also involves triangulation, i.e., harmonizing or even producing new statistics that reconcile various data sources. Results can lead to more timely and relevant statistics that can yield granular aggregated data in a cost-effective manner.

NSO = national statistics office.

[a] Relevance of statistics pertains to whether the data producer is producing information on the right topics and utilizing the appropriate concepts for measurement within these topics (Brackstone 1999).

continued on next page

Box 7 *continued*

[b]   Accuracy is largely whether estimates are of sufficient precision, i.e., whether they fall within an acceptable margin of error (Brackstone 1999).

[c]   Timeliness relates to when statistical information is made available to clients of data producers (Brackstone 1999).

[d]   As pointed out in Brackstone (1999): "For statistical information to be useful, clients have to be able to determine what is available and how they could obtain it. It then has to be available to potential clients in a form that they can use and afford. Both searching facilities and statistical products themselves have to use technology that is available to potential clients. This collection of considerations will be referred to as accessibility."

[e]   According to Brackstone (1999): "To make appropriate use of statistical information from the NSO clients have to know what they have and to understand the properties of the information. That requires the NSO to provide descriptions of the underlying concepts, variables and classifications that have been used, the methods of collection, processing and estimation used in producing the information, and its own assessment of the accuracy of the information. We will refer to this property of statistical information as its interpretability."

[f]   Coherence is "the degree to which statistical information fits into broad frameworks and uses standard concepts, variables, classifications and methods" Brackstone (1999). Relevance of statistics pertains to whether the data producer is producing information on the right topics and utilizing the appropriate concepts for measurement within these topics (Brackstone 1999).

Source: United Nations Economic and Social Commission for Asia and the Pacific. 2020. *Asia-Pacific Guidelines to Data Integration for Official Statistics*. Bangkok. https://repository.unescap.org/bitstream/handle/20.500.12870/3539/ESCAP-2020-MN-Asia-Pacific-guidelines.pdf.

Some examples of how data integration is used as a tool to produce added value to administrative data are described in the following:

Colombia

As reported in the Inventory of Collaborative, the NSO of Colombia experimented with the production of statistics based on a data integration of the following administrative social registers: the social security register (of the Ministry of Public Health), the population register (of the NSO), and the statistical register of labor relations (based on the administrative record of payments to the social security system.) Data integration was facilitated by the unique tax identification numbers of persons provided by the tax authority. Work streams involved data wrangling or cleaning and agreements on standards for the derived variables from the resulting integrated dataset. Quality criteria were established for production and release of the resulting statistics on payroll indicators; these criteria provided a means of examining gender wage gaps and informality in the labor market.

Estonia

In Estonia, the Youth Guarantee Support System, which commenced in 2018, integrates data from nine registers to identify and reach out to young people who are not engaged in education, employment or training and integrating them into the labor market (Kõiv 2018; OECD 2021). Data integrated from several administrative data sources generates data on rates of young people not engaged in education, employment, or training to help develop active labor market policies that reduce youth unemployment.

New Zealand

The Integrated Data Infrastructure (IDI) is a large research database curated by Statistics New Zealand (n.d.). It contains matched, de-identified data on people in New Zealand collected by various government agencies, as well as nongovernment organizations). The IDI contains longitudinal data on more than 9 million people on health, education and training, benefits and social services, justice, income and work, migration, and housing, among others. The IDI complements the Longitudinal Business Database, which holds linked microdata about businesses in New Zealand. The two separate databases are linked through tax data pertaining to individuals' and businesses' registration numbers.

Statistics New Zealand receives new data regularly and updates the IDI quarterly. When integrating new data into the IDI, Statistics New Zealand links each individual's records across multiple datasets before removing all identifiable features such as names. This allows data users to view de-identified records of individuals and interactions across services and government agencies. Any risk of the person being identified is minimized following the "five safes" framework that Statistics New Zealand uses to protect personal data in the IDI. Statistics New Zealand regularly checks linked records as part of its quality assurance. In cases where Statistics New Zealand is unable to find an individual's exact match across tables, it uses use probabilistic linking. This involves finding the closest possible match using all available information.

The IDI can be accessed from secure environments called "data labs." Organizations may apply to Statistics New Zealand to set up their own data lab if they intend to use the IDI for a prolonged period of time. Access to Stats NZ microdata is granted only after research proposals are assessed against the Ngā Tikanga Paihere and 5 Safes frameworks. These frameworks are used to evaluate appropriate engagement with the communities the researchers are studying – ensuring ethical and culturally appropriate use of the microdata, as well as protecting the privacy of those represented in the data. Figure 8 is a schematic showing the linkage between the IDI and the Longitudinal Business Database.

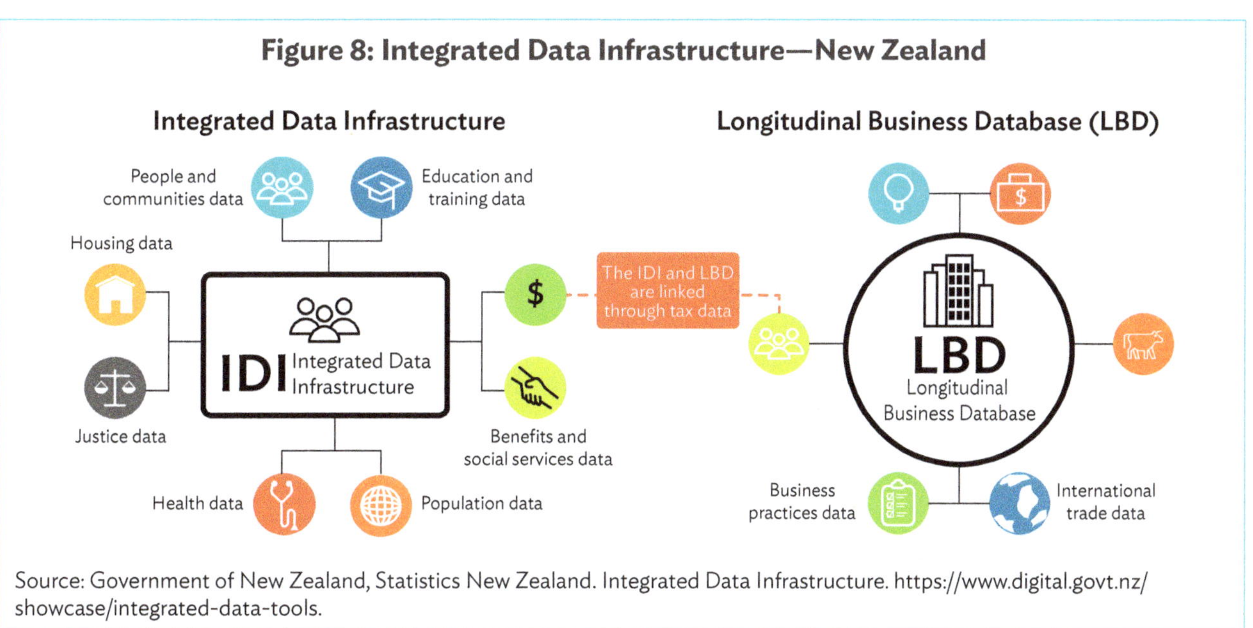

Source: Government of New Zealand, Statistics New Zealand. Integrated Data Infrastructure. https://www.digital.govt.nz/showcase/integrated-data-tools.

VII. Resources Developing Methods and Building Capacity in Using Administrative Data

NSOs have increasingly recognized the importance of using administrative data to meet demands for statistics. This section highlights the priority needs and needed actions for strengthening capacity to harness data from the administrative systems that produce them, specifically for NSOs in Asia and the Pacific. The chapter concludes with a resources list that provide information on capacity-building initiatives and related knowledge products.

Needs for Capacity Building

While NSOs are also in need of capacity building activities to strengthen their administrative data systems, they recognize that other government offices need assistance in this area as well. Thus, several NSOs in Asia and the Pacific have started taking steps to support other offices in improving their collection of administrative data. Figure 9 shows that 11 NSOs have collaborated with other offices in conducting research studies on collection and/or use of administrative data. Nine NSOs have conducted advocacy activities, eight have supported the establishment of a statistical unit in other offices, and seven have conducted regular trainings for staff of other offices.

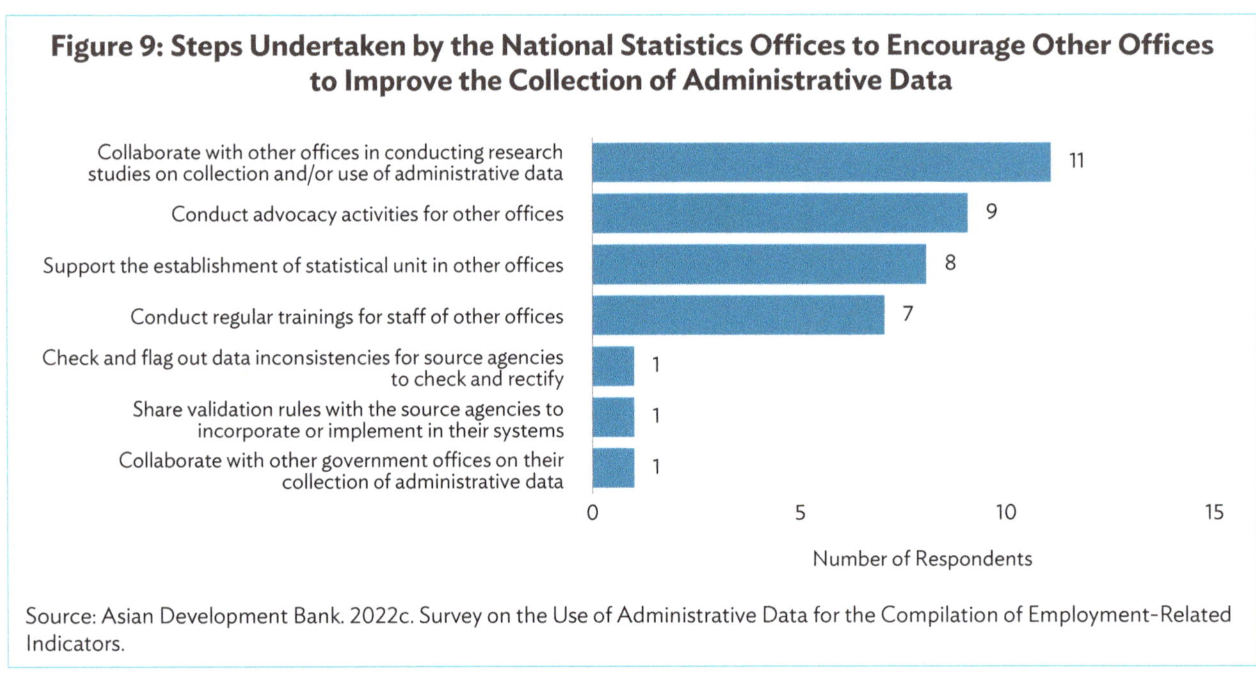

Figure 9: Steps Undertaken by the National Statistics Offices to Encourage Other Offices to Improve the Collection of Administrative Data

Source: Asian Development Bank. 2022c. Survey on the Use of Administrative Data for the Compilation of Employment-Related Indicators.

Almost half (45.8%) of NSOs in Asia and the Pacific that responded to ADB's SUADCEI 2022 have plans to expand the collection of administrative data. As summarized in Figure 10, 54.5% plan to expand examination of administrative data sources and 27.3% intend to engage in data integration tasks.

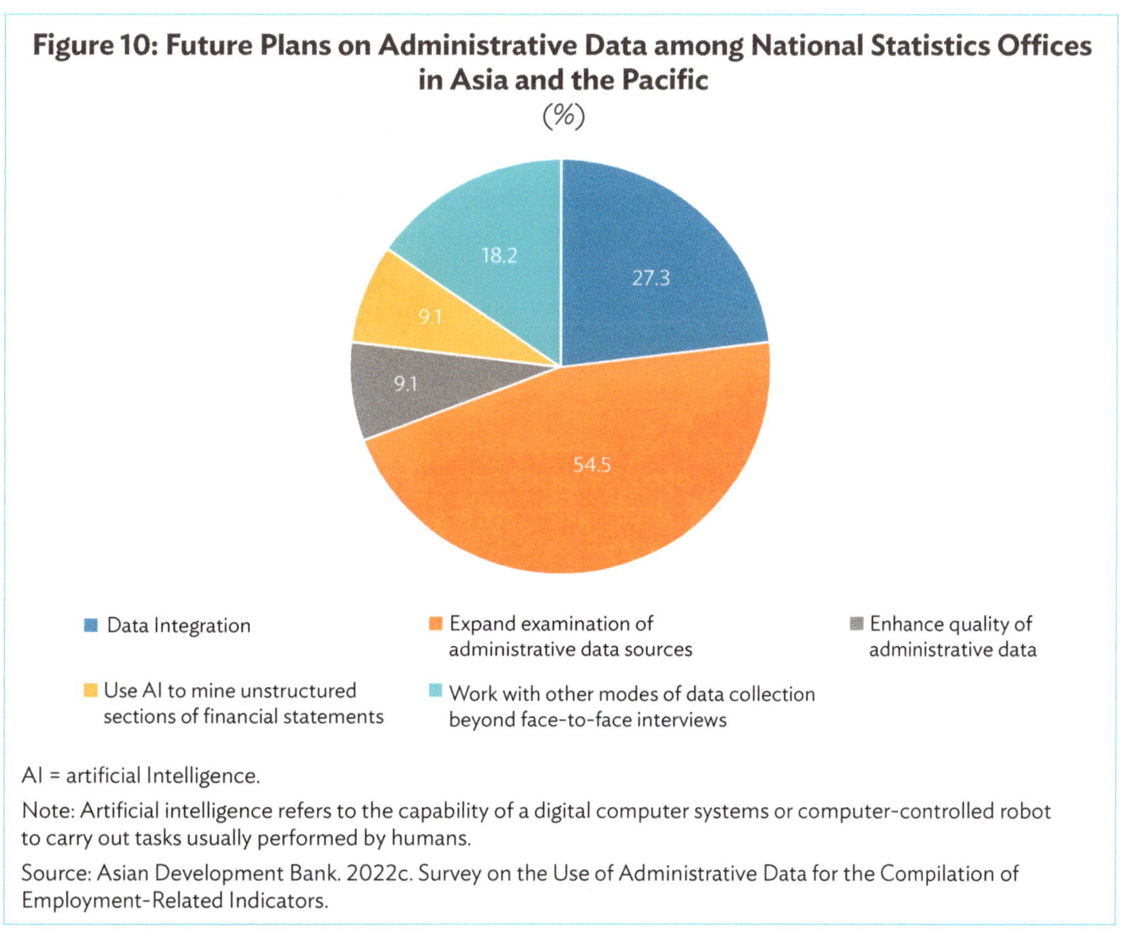

Figure 10: Future Plans on Administrative Data among National Statistics Offices in Asia and the Pacific

(%)

AI = artificial Intelligence.

Note: Artificial intelligence refers to the capability of a digital computer systems or computer-controlled robot to carry out tasks usually performed by humans.

Source: Asian Development Bank. 2022c. Survey on the Use of Administrative Data for the Compilation of Employment-Related Indicators.

Figure 10 summarizes specific actions identified by government agencies with plans for strengthening the use of administrative data; 25 agencies identified the need for establishment of statistical database or register and for more partnerships with other government agencies, while 24 agencies proposed regular updating of administrative data.

These actions can be mapped into the steps of the broad road map for enhanced access to administrative data sources by NSOs described in this section.

Resources

Global, regional, and national explorations and applications to improve use of administrative data to produce official statistics are described in this section. Implementation mechanisms and knowledge products of these initiatives are likewise documented in accessible formats, in addition to those cited in the respective sections of this report.

(i)   **The Administrative Data Collaborative**

The United Nations Statistics Division and the Global Partnership for Sustainable Development Data convened in May 2020 a multi-stakeholder collaborative of national statistics offices and regional and international agencies (called the Collaborative on Use of Administrative Data for Statistics) that aims to respond to urgent and longer-term needs to increase use of administrative data for statistical purposes. The COVID-19 pandemic highlighted the urgent need for better statistics on the population in the absence of surveys and censuses as well as the need for online sharing of experiences, best practices, and capacity building.

This Collaborative on Use of Administrative Data for Statistics has since become a dynamic platform for exchanging of resources, instruments, best practices, and experiences, and for increasing understanding among the national statistical systems about the merits of sharing and integrating administrative sources to enhance the quality, timeliness, coverage, and granularity of statistical data. Resources are developed collaboratively by members of the collaborative. To ensure that the guidance and training materials are readily applicable in a broad range of settings and national contexts, the Collaborative includes technical experts from over 25 NSOs of developed and developing countries and it draws on the expertise of 20 United Nations regional and specialized agencies and other organizations and initiatives. The developmental work is tasked to three teams: (i) task team 1, which is responsible for institutional framework, coordination, and partnerships; (ii) task team 2, which is responsible for data management and standardization; and (iii) task team 3, which is responsible for technical interoperability and linking.

The collaborative has also organized "expert clinics"[5] that focus on concrete, more specialized topics defined by members' needs, and is designed to facilitate "exchange of experiences, to inspire each other and find solutions together." The first in the series (four clinics were conducted in 2021) was an expert clinic on labor statistics. In 2022, the collaborative worked with a number of countries to promote collaboration with administrative data owners. These experiences were presented at a side event of the 54th session of the United Nations Statistical Commission.[6]

The website of the collaborative makes print materials readily available and easy to find through an inventory listing[7] that is kept updated. The materials (available in four languages—English, French, Norwegian, and Spanish) are grouped into nine themes, including a labor theme, and categorized by six types of materials: (i) case studies, (ii) e-learning or webinars, (iii) international guidelines, (iv) reports, (v) seminars and workshops, and (vi) tools. In addition, materials can be accessed by the nature of the type of guidance needed: coordination and collaboration, data quality, dissemination, governance, information technology, interoperability, linking, privacy and security, and standards and metadata.

Discussions on more general or cross-cutting topics are also documented and disseminated through the webinars and event pages of the website. Further, blogs are shared by UNSD and the Global Partnership for Sustainable Development Data on their websites.

---

5   UNSD and GPSDD. Collaborative on the Use of Administrative Data for Statistics: Expert Clinics. https://unstats.un.org/UNSDWebsite/capacity-development/admin-data/clinic/.

6   The video can be accessed here: UNSD. Advances in Strengthening Administrative Data for Official Statistics Side Event at the 54th session of the United Nations Statistical Commission. https://unstats.un.org/UNSDWebsite/events-details/un54sc-27022023-strengthening-administrative-data.

7   UNSD and GPSDD. Inventory listing. https://unstats.un.org/UNSDWebsite/capacity-development/admin-data/inventory.

(ii)   **Asian Development Bank Initiatives**

ADB has taken a number of initiatives in support of the use of administrative data for the compilation of development indicators.

(a)   The Administrative Data Sources for Compiling Millennium Development Goals and Related Indicators is a reference handbook that features practices and experiences on the use of data from education, health, and vital registration systems.

(b)   Preparing a Road Map on the Use of Administrative Data for Compiling Employment Statistics presents key factors on how to leverage administrative data to monitor development indicators in the labor sector. It also describes initiatives undertaken by selected economies in Asia and the Pacific.

(c)   Harnessing Administrative Data for Evidence-Based Labor Policy Making discusses how administrative data can aid in the production of more high-quality, detailed, timely, and relevant information when integrated in other data sources, which can help develop policies that are efficient and responsive to the needs of workers.

(d)   Practical Guidebook on Data Disaggregation for the Sustainable Development Goals, among others, presents the advantages, potentials, and drawbacks of different data sources, including administrative reporting systems.

(e)   A Gender-Sensitive Earthquake Recovery Assessment Using Administrative and Satellite Data: The Case of Indonesia's 2016 Aceh Earthquake is a study that used administrative data, along with satellite data, to evaluate the medium-term recovery of women after the 2016 Aceh earthquake at the village level.

(f)   Mapping the Spatial Distribution of Poverty Using Satellite Imagery in Thailand used a method where survey data were combined with data from other data sources such as administrative data sources to generate more granular poverty estimates.

(iii)   **Others**

Other international organizations have also made contributions in strengthening the use of administrative data as a data source in the region by publishing several knowledge products. These include the following:

(a)   Guidelines on the Use of Registers and Administrative Data
(b)   Quick Guide on Sources and Uses of Labor Statistics
(c)   Compilation and Presentation of Labor Statistics Based on Administrative Records
(d)   Re-using Administrative Data for Statistics: Case Studies from Five Countries
(e)   Tapping into administrative data in census-taking: an emerging trend in Asia and the Pacific
(f)   Administrative data systems versus prevalence surveys: Are they equally suited to give us data on the prevalence of violence against women?
(g)   Labor Statistics Based on Administrative Records: Guidelines on compilation and presentation.

Final Notes

NSOs are the key players in producing labor and employment statistics from administrative data. They have in place some prerequisites, such as legislation, staff skills for data curation, and confidentiality tools. Moreover, NSOs have built trust among citizens with their experience in the conduct of statistical activities that ensure confidentiality of information. Being the custodian of the population census dataset and the establishment census dataset, NSOs also have experience in the processing and analysis of data, as well as in the assurance of data quality. But NSOs are not the only actors in the labor and employment data ecosystem. NSOs must work together with line ministries to identify administrative data registers or systems that can be used to complement conventional data sources for work-, employment-, and other development-related indicators.

Effective and sustained capacity building is needed. This entails long-term structural investments and real knowledge transfer, as well as transformation of the enabling environment, institutions, and people behind the institutions. NSOs and data owners will need their staff members to develop new skill sets (encompassing both technical and soft skills) that enable them to harness new technologies, apply complex statistical methodologies, collaborate to understand legal and policy issues, and effectively communicate and negotiate.

Administrative data should be used effectively. Ultimately, administrative data, given its strengths and limitations, should be harnessed to describe the labor market, inform policy formulation, enable policy evaluation, and allow for macroeconomic monitoring. Labor and employment statistics have a very wide scope to describe, covering both labor supply and labor demand and governance, the micro and the macro levels, and all actors (individuals, businesses, and the public sector) in the labor market. Insights gained can help develop sustainable policies and actions to foster an environment that can create full and productive employment, and decent work for all.

Glossary

Accessibility – data readily located and accessed within a specific platform. Information should be available to users that is both useful and affordable (Brackstone 1999).

Accuracy – level to which the data correctly estimate or present the characteristics or quantities they are devised to gauge. Estimates are considered of sufficient precision when they are within an allowable "margin of error" (Brackstone 1999).

Active labor market policies – policies on the labor market that stimulate employment and creation of jobs through vocational training, provision of hiring subsidies, public work programs, and promotion of self-employment and small- and medium-sized enterprises.

Administrative data – data sourced from administrative records collected by a government ministry, department or agency primarily for administrative (not research or statistical) purposes. These administrative purposes are related to the corresponding executive or lawful functions such as authorizations, registrations, permits, payments, sanctions, control etc. Administrative data may include both data in administrative registers and data in other administrative sources (UNSD 2018).

(Administrative) register – a record of specific population that is maintained as a basic source of public administration.

Big data – fast growing large datasets with various formats that are regarded as by-products resulting from the utilization of tools in information and technology.

Child labor – the engagement of children in work or activities that could affect their mental, physical, social, and/or educational development.

Coherence – when data are mutually consistent and connected logically. It implies that data are based on common concepts, definitions, and methodologies.

Cost-efficiency – the burden of cost and provider relative to the data.

Credibility – the trust that users put in the data depending on the reputation of the source. It is part of the integrity of the process of production.

Data integration – combination of activities to merge data from various sources into significant and valuable information. It can include data consolidation from different sources, geospatial alongside statistical or non-statistical data, data pooling, record matching or linkage, data fusion, or data prioritization (UNESCAP 2020).

Data quality – multifaceted concept that consists of eight dimensions for consideration: accessibility, accuracy, coherence, credibility, interpretability, relevance, timeliness, and cost-efficiency (OECD 2017).

Decent work – work that is productive, protects rights, and has appropriate pay and social protection. It also indicates wide access to earning opportunities.

Displaced workers – workers who have suffered job loss because of downsizing and/or closure of firms.

Employed – working-aged persons who, in a certain reference period (at least 1 hour in a period of 1 week or 7 days), are occupied in any work done (involving the provision of goods or services), for remuneration.

Employees – those who are engaged in paid employment jobs.

Employers – workers either own account and/or with one or more partners whose remuneration depend on the profits produced from services and goods and have one or two employees.

Forced labor – work done against one's will under threat of any penalty.

Gender wage gap – difference between the median wages of women and men relative to the median of wages of men.

Geospatial data – information on events, objects, or phenomena that are location or take place on the earth's surface. It combines location data (coordinates on the earth), attribute (characteristics), and temporal (time or life span) information.

Gig workers – this is also known as platform workers, the vital component of this type of worker is the digital labor platforms on which jobs are outsourced to individuals in a specific location. Characterized by those who work temporary jobs in single projects or tasks typically in the service sector.

Global supply chains – organization of cross-border activities that engage in the production of services and goods brought to consumers through inputs and various stages of development, production, and delivery.

Green jobs – jobs that help preserve and restore the environment through protection and restoration of ecosystems, reduction of energy and raw material consumption, minimization of waste and pollution, and limiting of emissions of greenhouse gases.

Inclusive growth – growth of the economy that provides opportunities for everyone and is fairly allocated across society.

Informal economy – encompasses economic activities without formal regulation and/or not covered with enough labor legislation, wages, benefits, and taxes.

Informal employment – jobs that lack employment benefits and legal and social protection. This includes own-account workers, employers and members of producers' cooperatives employed in their own informal sector enterprises; own-account workers that produce goods exclusive for own use by their household; contributing family workers (family members who help with the business, with or without pay); and employees with informal jobs.

Informal sector – comprised of small, unregistered, unincorporated private enterprises, sometimes partly, involved in producing goods and providing services. Small enterprises have fewer regular employees than the number set by an economy. Unregistered enterprises are those not registered and not covered by commercial acts, social security or tax laws, or regulations by professional associations. Enterprises that are unincorporated usually do not have a complete set of accounts.

International labor standards – an extensive system of instruments on social policy and work, supported by a supervising system that addresses problems in application at the national level.

Interpretability – the ease with which users can properly use, understand, and analyze data. The degree of interpretability depends on the adequacy of target populations, definitions of variables and concepts, information on limitations, and the terminology underlying the data.

Labor force – total number of employed and unemployed.

Labor force participation rate – share of working-age population that are part of the labor market either looking for work or by working; it indicates the supply of labor available in producing goods and services.

Labor income – includes the amount earned by employees from working and a portion of the income of the self-employed.

Labor market outcomes – improved access and quality of employment.

Labor market programs – include trainings, direct job creations, public employment services, hiring subsidies, and unemployment benefits.

Labor migration – involves workers that contribute to development and growth in their destination economies, while their economies of origin gain from the remittances and acquired skills.

Labor share of gross domestic product – percentage of total compensation of employees in relation to gross domestic product.

Labor utilization – mean number of working hours per year, per head of the population.

Longitudinal information – information that provides a life-course perspective to analysis.

Non-formal education and training – education for all ages that take place inside and outside educational institutions.

Occupational injuries – disease, death, or any personal injury resulting from an occupational accident.

Old-age pension – contributory schemes and/or a mix of contributory and noncontributory schemes with the goal of giving older people income security.

Older persons – persons aged 60 years and older.

Own-account workers – self-employed workers without formal work arrangements and employees aside from family members who help out without receiving salary.

Part-time employment – employment involving jobs with fewer working hours than comparable full-time employment.

Persons with disabilities – those whose physical, mental, intellectual, or sensory impairments may hinder their effective and full involvement in society on an equal basis with others.

Persons outside the labor force – persons who are neither employed nor unemployed.

Poverty line – a threshold set by the World Bank that classifies people whose income fall below the threshold as poor. People are considered in extreme poverty when their income fall below $2.15 per day.

Productive employment – jobs that offer enough pay to fund the basic needs of workers and their dependents.

Relevance – reflects the degree to which data meets the needs of users. It pertains to whether the data producer is producing information on the right topics and utilizing the appropriate concepts for measurement within these topics (Brackstone 1999).

Small area estimates – estimates derived using a set of techniques applied by national statistics offices and other organizations to derive more granular and quality estimates appropriate for publication.

Self-employed – workers whose jobs fall under the following categories: own-account workers, contributing family workers, employers, and members of producers' cooperatives.

Social assistance – a form of social protection funded from the general government's revenue rather than individual contributions. This assistance encompasses programs that benefit households or individuals under a certain income threshold, or that target specific groups such as poor people, older people, and children.

Social benefits – benefits given in kind or in cash for needs arising from events that may have detrimental effects on the well-being of a household and its members (e.g., sickness, retirement, unemployment, education, and housing).

Social insurance – social security benefits funded by contributions (shared by workers and employers) and sometimes subsidies from government revenue. These benefits include health insurance, contributory pensions, and other schemes such as provident funds, unemployment insurance, and work insurance schemes.

Social pension – tax funded cash transfers for older people with the aim of giving income security in old age.

Social protection – benefits provided by an economy for poor people, the sick, persons with disability, jobless persons, older people, the young, and dependents through a social security system, private insurance, personal savings, social customs and relief organizations, or through combined sources.

Timeliness – the duration of time between when data becomes available and the events to which they pertain. It is assessed based on the time period that allows the data to be of value.

Underemployment – workers who are willing and able to work more than the number of hours they are currently working based on a certain threshold of working hours.

Unemployed – includes persons of working age without work, those who have sought work in the recent past, and those who are currently available for work.

Unemployment rate – share of the number of unemployed in relation to the total labor force.

Vulnerable employment – employment involving workers who are own-account workers and/or contributing family members.

Working-age persons – people 15 years of age and older. The lower age limit set by the International Labour Organization is 15.

Working poor – workers whose incomes are too low and/or those who cannot get enough work to get themselves and their families out of poverty.

Youth – generally refers to those aged 15–24 years, though definitions vary across Asia and the Pacific. The Asian Development Bank defines youth as those belonging to 18–29 years of age.

Youth not in employment, education, or training – young people who are either unemployed or inactive and not involved in education or training.

Youth unemployment – encompasses unemployed persons aged 15–24 years.

Appendixes

Appendix 1: Survey on the Use of Administrative Data for the Compilation of Employment-Related Indicators (For National Statistics Office)

*Required

Organization Information

1. Name of Government Ministry or Office*

2. Name of Head of Office*

3. Office Address*

4. Office Website*

5. Name of Focal Point or Contact Person*

6. Telephone Number*

7. Email Address*

Part I. Administrative Data Collection and Compilation

8. Does your office collect, compile, or consolidate administrative data for either statistical or nonstatistical use?
    - ☐ Yes (*Please proceed to Question 9*)
    - ☐ No (*Please proceed to Question 19*)

9.   What is/are the objective/s of your office in collecting administrative data? Please check all that apply.
     - ☐ To register important events, as mandated by law or relevant authorities (e.g., registry of person's birth, death, registry of business)
     - ☐ To deliver services (e.g., administer benefits such as aid, pensions, tax collection)
     - ☐ To monitor important transactions to be able to assess how the institution is achieving its intended goals
     - ☐ For other routine operations of the institution
     - ☐ For statistical purposes (e.g., develop sampling frame, compile official statistics)
     - ☐ Others (please specify) __________________________________

10. Is any of administrative data that your office collects, compiles, or consolidates being used as inputs by other government offices to design or evaluate policies?
     - ☐ Yes, other government offices use the administrative data that our office collects, compiles, or consolidates to design or evaluate policies. (*Please proceed to Question 11*)
     - ☐ No, other government offices do not use the administrative data that our office collects, compiles, or consolidates to design or evaluate policies. (*Please proceed to Question 12*)

11. Kindly check all the policy uses below for which other government offices apply the administrative data that you collect.
     - ☐ Economic policies
     - ☐ Labor policies
     - ☐ Education policies
     - ☐ Health policies
     - ☐ Social protection policies
     - ☐ Finance policies (e.g., on tax)
     - ☐ Others (please specify) __________________________________

12. Are any of the administrative data that your office collects, compiles, or consolidates used to compile any work, labor, and/or employment-related indicators or statistics? Please check all that apply.
     - ☐ Yes, they are used to compile employment-related Sustainable Development Goal (SDG) indicator/s. (*Please proceed to Question 13.*)
     - ☐ Yes, they are used to compile non-SDG indicator/s on work-, labor-, and/or employment-related topics. Please specify. ________________________ (*Please proceed to Question 14*)
     - ☐ No, the administrative data that our office collects are not used to compile any work-, labor-, and/or employment-related indicators or statistics. (*Please proceed to Question 14*)

13. Kindly specify the employment-related SDG indicator/s by checking all that apply below.
     - ☐ SDG 1.1.1 Proportion of the population living below the international poverty line by sex, age, employment status and geographic location (urban or rural)
     - ☐ SDG 1.3.1 Proportion of population covered by social protection floors or systems, by sex, distinguishing children, unemployed persons, older persons, persons with disabilities, pregnant women, newborns, work-injury victims, and the poor and the vulnerable
     - ☐ SDG 1.a.2 Proportion of total government spending on essential services (education, health, and social protection)
     - ☐ SDG 4.3.1 Participation rate of youth and adults in formal and nonformal education and training in the previous 12 months, by sex
     - ☐ SDG 5.5.2 Proportion of women in managerial positions
     - ☐ SDG 8.2.1 Annual growth rate of real gross domestic product per employed person

☐ SDG 8.3.1 Proportion of informal employment in total employment, by sector and sex
☐ SDG 8.5.1 Average hourly earnings of employees, by sex, age, occupation, and persons with disabilities
☐ SDG 8.5.2 Unemployment rate, by sex, age, and persons with disabilities
☐ SDG 8.6.1 Proportion of youth (aged 15–24 years) not in education, employment, or training
☐ SDG 8.7.1 Proportion and number of children aged 5–17 years engaged in child labor, by sex and age
☐ SDG 8.8.1 Fatal and nonfatal occupational injuries per 100,000 workers, by sex and migrant status
☐ SDG 8.8.2 Level of national compliance with labor rights (freedom of association and collective bargaining) based on International Labour Organization (ILO) textual sources and national legislation, by sex and migrant status
☐ SDG 8.b.1 Existence of a developed and operationalized national strategy for youth employment, as a distinct strategy or as part of a national employment strategy
☐ SDG 10.4.1 Labor share of gross domestic product
☐ SDG 10.7.1 Recruitment cost borne by employee as a proportion of monthly income earned in country of destination
☐ SDG 14.c.1 Number of countries making progress in ratifying, accepting, and implementing through legal, policy and institutional frameworks, ocean-related instruments that implement international law, as reflected in the United Nations Convention on the Law of the Sea, for the conservation, and sustainable use of the oceans and their resources
☐ SDG 16.10.1 Number of verified cases of killing, kidnapping, enforced disappearance, arbitrary detention, and torture of journalists, associated media personnel, trade unionists, and human rights advocates in the previous 12 months
☐ Others (please specify) [   ]

14. Is your office aware of other datasets (both administrative or nonadministrative data, e.g., surveys) that could be potentially integrated with the administrative data identified earlier to address any of the issues on granularity, timeliness, spatial comparability, and comparability over time? Please check all that apply.
    ☐ Yes, our office collects other administrative or nonadministrative data that can be integrated to address the issues identified. (*Please proceed to Question 15*)
    ☐ Yes, other government offices collect data that can be integrated to address the issues identified. (*Please proceed to Question 15*)
    ☐ Yes, other nongovernment offices (e.g., private sector, nongovernment organizations, citizen-generated data) collect data that can be integrated to address the issues identified. (*Please proceed to Question 15*)
    ☐ No, our office is not aware of any other data set that can be integrated to address the issues identified. (*Please proceed to Question 17*)

15. Is your office already integrating these data?
    ☐ Yes (*Please proceed to Question 17*)
    ☐ No (*Please proceed to Question 16*)

16. What are the reasons your office is not integrating these data? Please check all that apply.
    ☐ The technical capability of our staff needs to be enhanced in order to perform data integration.
    ☐ Our office lacks the needed infrastructure (computer hardware and software, networking servers, etc.).
    ☐ Our office does not consider data integration as urgent or necessary.
    ☐ Others (please specify)

17. Do you have access to the administrative data collected by other government offices that would potentially be useful to address the issues identified?
- ☐ Yes (*Please proceed to Question 19*)
- ☐ No (*Please proceed to Question 18*)

18. What prevents your office from securing access to these data? Please check all that apply.
- ☐ There are relevant law stipulations that make it challenging to get access to administrative data compiled by other government offices.
- ☐ We need a formal agreement / partnership with other government offices before we can access administrative data, but it takes time / challenging to have such formal partnership.
- ☐ When sharing data across offices, there are concerns on data confidentiality and security that are difficult to navigate.
- ☐ The need for data sharing is not urgent.
- ☐ Others (please specify)

Part II. COVID-19 Pandemic-Related Experiences on the Collection of Administrative Data

19. What are the impacts of the coronavirus disease (COVID-19) pandemic on your data collection activities? Please check all that apply.
- ☐ Our data collection activities (including surveys, censuses, updating of administrative data) have to be rescheduled, postponed, or canceled because of restrictions on movements of people.
- ☐ Our data collection activities (including surveys, censuses, updating of administrative data) have to be rescheduled, postponed, or cancelled to reallocate resources for other COVID-19 pandemic-related response.
- ☐ Our data collection activities (including surveys, censuses, updating of administrative data) have resorted to other ways of collecting data (e.g., shifting from face-to-face interviews, field data collection to phone-based, web or electronic-based, and/or other hybrid approaches of data collection).
- ☐ New and/or expanded data collection activities were initiated by our office (e.g., added questions on existing surveys and/or censuses; increased frequency or periodicity of existing surveys and/or censuses; increased sample size of existing surveys and/or censuses; collected new surveys to collect COVID-19 pandemic-related information.)
- ☐ Increased reliance on information available from existing administrative data collected by our office.
- ☐ Increased reliance on information available from existing administrative data collected by other government office.
- ☐ Increased reliance on alternative sources of data from non-government organizations (e.g., big data collected by private sector.)
- ☐ Others (please specify) [   ]

20. Did you encounter any issue in accessing and/or using information from administrative data that you think will be useful during the pandemic?
- ☐ Yes (*Please proceed to Question 21*)
- ☐ No (*Please proceed to Question 22*)

21. What issues did your office encounter in collecting and/or using administrative data during the pandemic? Please check all that apply.
- ☐ Access to administrative data requires office-level agreements.
- ☐ Administrative data collected by our office are not consolidated in a database.

☐ There are concerns on data quality affecting reliable statistical analysis (e.g., comparability across space and/or time).
☐ Incomplete coverage of data (e.g., data available for selected geographical areas or population group only).
☐ Disruption in office operations because of lockdowns and restrictions.
☐ Inadequate access to necessary information technology infrastructure (e.g., for work-from-home setup or remote access).
☐ Lack of human resources in compilation.
☐ Others (please specify) [   ]

22. In the wake of the restrictions during the pandemic, has your office opted to use administrative data to supplement the labor force survey (LFS) or any employment-related survey?
☐ Yes (*Please proceed to Question 23*)
☐ No (*Please proceed to Question 27*)

23. Kindly provide the data source of the administrative data used to supplement the LFS or any employment-related survey (e.g., Philippines' Department of Labor and Employment online Establishment Report System).
[   ]

24. Kindly provide the name of the office that compiles the administrative data used to supplement the LFS or any employment-related survey (e.g., Department of Labor and Employment).
[   ]

25. Kindly specify the report/s providing details on how the LFS or any employment-related data was supplemented with administrative data.
[   ]

26. Kindly provide the reason why the LFS or any employment-related survey was not supplemented with administrative data (e.g., the LFS covers informal sector employment so online registries of establishments do not sufficiently cover the employed population).
[   ]

27. Did your office collect administrative data from specific groups of workers (e.g., gig workers) and/or business sectors that were severely affected by the COVID-19 pandemic to contribute to designing policies?
☐ Yes (*Please proceed to Question 28*)
☐ No (*Please proceed to Question 31*)

28. Please specify the administrative data collected from specific groups of workers and/or business sectors that were severely affected by the COVID-19 pandemic.
[   ]

29. Please provide the source of the administrative data collected from specific groups of workers and/or business sectors that were severely affected by the COVID-19 pandemic.
[   ]

30. Please provide the website link to the report/s that describe/s the administrative data collected from specific groups of workers and/or business sectors.

[ ]

Part III. Initiatives to Enhance the Collection and Use of Administrative Data

31. Does your office have plans or initiatives to expand the collection of administrative data?
    - ☐ Yes (*Please proceed to Question 32*)
    - ☐ No (*Please proceed to Question 36*)

32. Please provide details of your office's plans and/or initiatives on the expansion of collection of administrative data (e.g., innovations in data collection).

[ ]

33. Proposed date of launch (if not yet launched) or actual date of launch (if already started).

[ ]

34. Specific purpose of the initiative.

[ ]

35. Status.
    - ☐ Planning stage.
    - ☐ Ongoing.
    - ☐ Completed.

36. Does your office encourage other offices (data owners) to improve the collection of administrative data?
    - ☐ Yes (*Please proceed to Question 37*)
    - ☐ No

37. What steps has your office undertaken to encourage other offices to improve the collection of administrative data? Please check all that apply.
    - ☐ Conduct of advocacy activities for other offices on enhancing the collection of administrative data for statistical purposes
    - ☐ Conduct of regular trainings (e.g., on data collection, data quality assessment, etc.) for staff of other offices
    - ☐ Collaborate with other offices in conducting (in house and outsourced) research studies on collection / use of administrative data
    - ☐ Support the establishment of statistical unit in every government / non-government office collecting administrative data
    - ☐ Others (please specify) [ ]

38. What actions do you propose to improve and strengthen the use of administrative data? Please check all that apply.
    - ☐ Establish a statistical database or register that is readily accessible to users.
    - ☐ Ensure regular updating of administrative data.

- ☐ Improve data quality to allow for reliable statistical analysis (e.g., comparability across space and/or time.) (Comparability implies that the data are based on common concepts, definitions, and methods across location or over time, or that any differences are explained and can be allowed for.)
- ☐ Improve coverage and granularity of data (implies that the data sufficiently represent samples from each subgroup of the population or each geographic area).
- ☐ Conduct training on data analytics.
- ☐ Conduct (in-house and outsourced) research studies on use of administrative data.
- ☐ Explore innovative dissemination practices (e.g., through social media and other online platforms).
- ☐ Establish more partnerships with other government offices.
- ☐ Simplify data sharing protocols.
- ☐ Strengthen data confidentiality.
- ☐ Others (please specify).

Appendix 2: Survey on the Use of Administrative Data for the Compilation of Employment-Related Indicators (For Labor Ministries)

Required

Organization Information

1. Name of Government Ministry or Office*

2. Name of Head of Office*

3. Office Address*

4. Office Website*

5. Name of Focal Point or Contact Person*

6. Telephone Number*

7. Email Address*

Part I. Administrative Data Collection and Compilation

8. Does your office collect, compile, or consolidate administrative data for either statistical or nonstatistical use?
    - ☐ Yes (*Please proceed to Question 9*)
    - ☐ No (*Please proceed to Question 15*)

9. What is/are the objective/s of your office in collecting, compiling, or consolidating administrative data? Please check all that apply.
    - ☐ To register important events, as mandated by law or relevant authorities (e.g., registry of person's birth, death; registry of business).
    - ☐ To deliver services (e.g., administer benefits such as aid, pensions, tax collection).
    - ☐ To monitor important transactions to be able to assess how the institution is achieving its intended goals.
    - ☐ For other routine operations of the institution.
    - ☐ For statistical purposes (e.g., compile official statistics).
    - ☐ Others (please specify)

10. Is any of administrative data which your office collects, compiles, or consolidates being used as inputs by other government offices to design or evaluate policies?
    - ☐ Yes, other government offices use the administrative data that our office collects, compiles, or consolidates to design or evaluate policies. (*Please proceed to Question 11*)
    - ☐ No, I am not aware of other policy uses of administrative data that our office collects, compiles, or consolidates to design or evaluate policies. (*Please proceed to Question 12*)

11. Kindly check all policies that apply.
    - ☐ Economic policies
    - ☐ Labor policies
    - ☐ Education policies
    - ☐ Health policies
    - ☐ Social protection policies
    - ☐ Finance policies (e.g., on tax)
    - ☐ Others (please specify) [____________________]

12. Are any of the administrative data that your office collects, compiles, or consolidates used to compile any work-, labor-, and/or employment-related indicators or statistics?
    - ☐ Yes, they are used to compile employment-related Sustainable Development Goal indicator/s. (*Please proceed to Question 13*)
    - ☐ Yes, they are used to compile non-SDG indicator/s on work, labor, and/or employment related topics. (*Please proceed to Question 14*)
    - ☐ No, the administrative data that our office collects are not used to compile any work, labor, and/or employment-related indicators or statistics. (*Please proceed to Question 14*)

13. Kindly specify the employment-related SDG indicator/s by checking all that apply.
    - ☐ SDG 1.1.1 Proportion of the population living below the international poverty line by sex, age, employment status and geographic location (urban or rural)
    - ☐ SDG 1.3.1 Proportion of population covered by social protection floors or systems, by sex, distinguishing children, unemployed persons, older persons, persons with disabilities, pregnant women, newborns, work-injury victims, and the poor and the vulnerable
    - ☐ SDG 1.a.2 Proportion of total government spending on essential services (education, health, and social protection)
    - ☐ SDG 4.3.1 Participation rate of youth and adults in formal and nonformal education and training in the previous 12 months, by sex
    - ☐ SDG 5.5.2 Proportion of women in managerial positions
    - ☐ SDG 8.2.1 Annual growth rate of real gross domestic product per employed person
    - ☐ SDG 8.3.1 Proportion of informal employment in nonagricultural employment, by sex; proportion of informal employment in total employment, by sector and sex
    - ☐ SDG 8.5.1 Average hourly earnings of female and male employees, by occupation, age, and persons with disabilities; average hourly earnings of employees, by sex, age, occupation, and persons with disabilities
    - ☐ SDG 8.5.2 Unemployment rate, by sex, age, and persons with disabilities
    - ☐ SDG 8.6.1 Proportion of youth (aged 15–24 years) not in education, employment, or training
    - ☐ SDG 8.7.1 Proportion and number of children aged 5–17 years engaged in child labor, by sex and age
    - ☐ SDG 8.8.1 Frequency rates of fatal and nonfatal occupational injuries, by sex, and migrant status; fatal and nonfatal occupational injuries per 100,000 workers, by sex and migrant status

□ SDG 8.8.2 Level of national compliance with labor rights (freedom of association and collective bargaining) based on ILO textual sources and national legislation, by sex and migrant status

□ SDG 8.b.1 Existence of a developed and operationalized national strategy for youth employment, as a distinct strategy or as part of a national employment strategy

□ SDG 10.4.1 Labor share of gross domestic product

□ SDG 10.7.1 Recruitment cost borne by employee as a proportion of monthly income earned in country of destination

□ SDG 14.c.1 Number of countries making progress in ratifying, accepting, and implementing through legal, policy and institutional frameworks, ocean-related instruments that implement international law, as reflected in the United Nations Convention on the Law of the Sea, for the conservation, and sustainable use of the oceans and their resources

□ SDG 16.10.1 Number of verified cases of killing, kidnapping, enforced disappearance, arbitrary detention, and torture of journalists, associated media personnel, trade unionists, and human rights advocates in the previous 12 months

□ Others. Please specify. [   ]

14. Is your office aware of other datasets (both administrative or nonadministrative data (e.g., surveys) that could be potentially integrated with the administrative data identified earlier to address any of the issues on granularity, timeliness, and comparability across economies and over time? Please check all that apply.

□ Yes, our office collects other administrative or non-administrative data that can be integrated to address any of the issues on granularity, timeliness, and comparability across economies and over time.

□ Yes, other government offices collect data that can be integrated to address any of the issues on granularity, timeliness, and comparability across economies and over time.

□ Yes, other nongovernment offices (e.g., private sector, nongovernment organizations, citizen-generated data) collect data that can be integrated to address any of the issues on granularity, timeliness, and comparability across economies and over time.

□ No, our office is not aware of any other data set that can be integrated to address any of the issues on granularity, timeliness, and comparability across economies and over time.

Part II. COVID-19 Pandemic-Related Experiences on the Collection and Use of Administrative Data

15. What are the impacts of the coronavirus disease (COVID-19) pandemic on your data collection activities? Please check all that apply.

□ Our data collection activities (e.g., updating of administrative data) have to be rescheduled, postponed, or canceled because of restrictions on movements of people. (*Please proceed to Question 17*)

□ Our data collection activities (e.g., updating of administrative data) have to be rescheduled, postponed, or canceled to reallocate resources for other COVID-19 pandemic-related responses. (*Please proceed to Question 17*)

□ Our data collection activities (e.g., updating of administrative data) have resorted to other ways of collecting data. (*Please proceed to Question 16*)

□ Others (please specify) [   ]

16. Please specify other ways of collecting data that your office has resort to.

[   ]

17. Did you encounter any issue in accessing and/or using information from administrative data that you think will be useful during the pandemic?
    □ Yes (*Please proceed to Question 18*)
    □ No (*Please proceed to Question 19*)

18. What issues did your office encounter in collecting and/or using administrative data during the pandemic? Please check all that apply.
    □ Access to administrative data requires office-level agreements.
    □ Administrative data collected by our office are not consolidated in a database-like format.
    □ Administrative data is not updated.
    □ There are concerns on data quality affecting reliable statistical analysis (e.g., comparability across space or time).
    □ Incomplete coverage of data (e.g., data available for selected geographical areas or population groups only).
    □ Disruption in office operations because of lockdowns and restrictions.
    □ Inadequate access to necessary information technology infrastructure (e.g., for work-from-home setup or remote access).
    □ Lack of human resources in compilation.
    □ Others (please specify) [   ]

19. In the wake of the restrictions during the pandemic, has your office opted to use administrative data to supplement your typical source of labor and employment statistics such as the labor force survey or any employment-related survey?
    □ Yes (*Please proceed to Question 20*)
    □ No (*Please proceed to Question 23*)

20. Kindly provide the data source of the administrative data.
    [   ]

21. Name of the office that compiles the administrative data.
    [   ]

22. State the report providing details on how the LFS or any employment-related data was supplemented with administrative data.
    [   ]

23. Did your office collect administrative data from specific groups of workers (e.g. gig workers) and/or business sectors that were severely affected by the COVID-19 pandemic to contribute to designing policies? (A gig worker is a person who works temporary jobs typically in the service sector as an independent contractor or freelancer.)
    □ Yes
    □ No

24. Please provide details of the administrative data collected from specific groups of workers and/or business sectors that were severely affected by the COVID-19 pandemic.
    [   ]

25. Source of administrative data.

26. Provide website link to report that explains administrative data collected from specific groups of workers and/or business sectors.

Part III. Initiatives to Enhance the Collection and Use of Administrative Data

27. Does your office have plans or initiatives to expand the collection of administrative data to supplement or enhance the current data portfolio that your office has?
    - ☐ Yes (*Please proceed to Question 28*)
    - ☐ No (*Please proceed to Question 32*)

28. Please provide details of your office's plans or initiatives on the expansion of collection of administrative data (e.g., innovations in data collection).

29. Proposed date of launch (if not yet launched) or actual date of launch (if already started).

30. Specific purpose of the initiative.

31. Status.
    - ☐ Planning stage.
    - ☐ Ongoing.
    - ☐ Completed.

32. What actions do you propose to improve and strengthen the use of administrative data? Please check all that apply.
    - ☐ Establish a statistical database or register that is readily accessible to users.
    - ☐ Ensure regular updating of administrative data.
    - ☐ Improve data quality to allow for reliable statistical analysis (e.g., comparability across space and/or time.) (*Comparability implies that the data are based on common concepts, definitions, and methods across location or over time, or that any differences are explained and can be allowed for.*)
    - ☐ Improve coverage and granularity of data (*implies that the data sufficiently represent samples from each subgroup of the population or each geographic area*).
    - ☐ Conduct training on data analytics.
    - ☐ Conduct (in-house and outsourced) research studies on use of administrative data.
    - ☐ Explore innovative dissemination practices (e.g., through social media and other online platforms).
    - ☐ More partnerships with other government offices.
    - ☐ Simplify data sharing protocols.
    - ☐ Strengthen data confidentiality.
    - ☐ Others (please specify)

33. Does your economy make use of a labor market information system?
    ☐ Yes (*Please proceed to Question 34*)
    ☐ No (End of survey)

34. Please provide the report that details the guidelines or quality assessment framework for administrative data used in the labor market information system. (You may provide the title of the report or the URL to the report if it is available online.)

Appendix 3: Survey on the Use of Administrative Data for the Compilation of Employment-Related Indicators (For Other Government Ministries or Offices)

***Required**

Organization Information

1. Name of Government Ministry or Office*

2. Name of Head of Office*

3. Office Address*

4. Office Website*

5. Name of Focal Point or Contact Person*

6. Telephone Number*

7. Email address*

Part I. Administrative Data Collection and Compilation

8. Does your office collect, compile, or consolidate administrative data for either statistical or nonstatistical use? (You will be directed to the next question based on your response).
    - ☐ Yes (*Please proceed to Question 9*)
    - ☐ No (*Please proceed to Question 49*)

9. What types of administrative data are being collected, compiled, or consolidated by your office? Please check all that apply.
    - ☐ Social security data (contributions, benefits, pensions)
    - ☐ Health records or registers
    - ☐ Education records or registers
    - ☐ Registration systems for persons (persons with disabilities [PWDs], unemployed, poor)
    - ☐ Register of farms
    - ☐ Telephone registry
    - ☐ Foreign trade registry
    - ☐ Border records

☐ Business registry
☐ Others (please specify) [   ]

10. What is/are the objective/s of your office in collecting, compiling, or consolidating administrative data? Please check all that apply.
    ☐ To register important events, as mandated by law or relevant authorities (e.g., registry of person's birth, death; registry of business).
    ☐ To deliver services (e.g., administer benefits such as aid, pensions, tax collection).
    ☐ To monitor important transactions to be able to assess how the institution is achieving its intended goals.
    ☐ For other routine operations of the institution.
    ☐ For statistical purposes (e.g., compile official statistics).
    ☐ Others (please specify) [   ]

11. Is any of administrative data that your office collects, compiles, or consolidates being used as inputs by other government offices to design or evaluate policies?
    ☐ Yes, other government offices use the administrative data that our office collects, compiles, or consolidates to design or evaluate policies. (*Please proceed to Question 12*)
    ☐ No, I am not aware of other policy uses of administrative data that our office collects, compiles or consolidates to design or evaluate policies. (*Please proceed to Question 13*)

12. Kindly check all policies that apply.
    ☐ Economic policies
    ☐ Labor policies
    ☐ Education policies
    ☐ Health policies
    ☐ Social protection policies
    ☐ Finance policies (e.g., on tax)
    ☐ Others (please specify) [   ]

13. Do the social security data that your office collect, compile, or consolidate provide comprehensive data or information on granularity or disaggregation?
(Granularity or disaggregation implies that the data sufficiently represent samples from each subgroup of the population or each geographic area.)
    ☐ Administrative data provide the required granularity.
    ☐ There is a need to enhance granularity.

14. Do the health records that your office collects, compiles, or consolidates provide comprehensive data or information on granularity or disaggregation?
(Granularity or disaggregation implies that the data sufficiently represent samples from each subgroup of the population or each geographic area.)
    ☐ Administrative data provide the required granularity.
    ☐ There is a need to enhance granularity.

15. Do the education records that your office collects, compiles, or consolidates provide comprehensive data or information on granularity and/or disaggregation?
    (Granularity or disaggregation implies that the data sufficiently represent samples from each subgroup of the population or each geographic area.)
    ☐ Administrative data provide the required granularity.
    ☐ There is a need to enhance granularity.

16. Do the registers for persons (persons with disabilities [PWDs], unemployed, poor) that your office collects, compiles, or consolidates provide comprehensive data or information on granularity or disaggregation?
    (Granularity or disaggregation implies that the data sufficiently represent samples from each subgroup of the population or each geographic area.)
    ☐ Administrative data provide the required granularity.
    ☐ There is a need to enhance granularity.

17. Do the registers for farms that your office collects, compiles, or consolidates provide comprehensive data or information on granularity or disaggregation?
    (Granularity or disaggregation implies that the data sufficiently represent samples from each subgroup of the population or each geographic area.)
    ☐ Administrative data provide the required granularity.
    ☐ There is a need to enhance granularity.

18. Do the telephone registers that your office collects, compiles, or consolidates provide comprehensive data or information on granularity or disaggregation?
    (Granularity or disaggregation implies that the data sufficiently represent samples from each subgroup of the population or each geographic area.)
    ☐ Administrative data provide the required granularity.
    ☐ There is a need to enhance granularity.

19. Do the foreign trade registers that your office collects, compiles, or consolidates provide comprehensive data or information on granularity or disaggregation?
    (Granularity or disaggregation implies that the data sufficiently represent samples from each subgroup of the population or each geographic area.)
    ☐ Administrative data provide the required granularity.
    ☐ There is a need to enhance granularity.

20. Do the border records that your office collects, compiles, or consolidates provide comprehensive data or information on granularity or disaggregation?
    (Granularity or disaggregation implies that the data sufficiently represent samples from each subgroup of the population or each geographic area.)
    ☐ Administrative data provide the required granularity.
    ☐ There is a need to enhance granularity.

21. Do the business registers that your office collects, compiles, or consolidates provide comprehensive data or information on granularity or disaggregation?
    (Granularity or disaggregation implies that the data sufficiently represent samples from each subgroup of the population or each geographic area.)
    ☐ Administrative data provide the required granularity.
    ☐ There is a need to enhance granularity.

22. Are the social security data that your office collects, compiles, or consolidates made available in a timely manner?
(Timeliness refers to the length of time between its availability and the event or phenomenon it describes.)
    - ☐ Yes
    - ☐ No

23. Are the health records that your office collects, compiles, or consolidates made available in a timely manner?
(Timeliness refers to the length of time between its availability and the event or phenomenon it describes.)
    - ☐ Yes
    - ☐ No

24. Are the education records that your office collects, compiles, or consolidates made available in a timely manner?
(Timeliness refers to the length of time between its availability and the event or phenomenon it describes.)
    - ☐ Yes
    - ☐ No

25. Are the registers for persons (PWDs, unemployed, poor) that your office collects, compiles, or consolidates made available in a timely manner?
(Timeliness refers to the length of time between its availability and the event or phenomenon it describes.)
    - ☐ Yes
    - ☐ No

26. Are the registers for farms that your office collects, compiles, or consolidates made available in a timely manner?
(Timeliness refers to the length of time between its availability and the event or phenomenon it describes.)
    - ☐ Yes
    - ☐ No

27. Are the telephone registers that your office collects, compiles, or consolidates made available in a timely manner?
(Timeliness refers to the length of time between its availability and the event or phenomenon it describes.)
    - ☐ Yes
    - ☐ No

28. Are the foreign trade registers that your office collects, compiles, or consolidates made available in a timely manner?
(Timeliness refers to the length of time between its availability and the event or phenomenon it describes.)
    - ☐ Yes
    - ☐ No

29. Are the border records that your office collects, compiles, or consolidates made available in a timely manner?
(Timeliness refers to the length of time between its availability and the event or phenomenon it describes.)
    - ☐ Yes
    - ☐ No

30. Are the business registries that your office collects, compiles, or consolidates made available in a timely manner?
    (Timeliness refers to the length of time between its availability and the event or phenomenon it describes.)
    - ☐ Yes
    - ☐ No

31. Are the social security data that your office collects, compiles, or consolidates spatially comparable with other economies?
    (Spatial comparability implies that, from economy to economy, the data are based on common concepts, definitions, classifications, and methodology, or that any differences are explained and can be allowed for.)
    - ☐ Yes
    - ☐ No

32. Are the health records that your office collects, compiles, or consolidates spatially comparable with other economies?
    (Spatial comparability implies that, from economy to economy, the data are based on common concepts, definitions, classifications and methodology, or that any differences are explained and can be allowed for.)
    - ☐ Yes
    - ☐ No

33. Are the education records that your office collects, compiles, or consolidates spatially comparable with other economies?
    (Spatial comparability implies that, from economy to economy, the data are based on common concepts, definitions, classifications and methodology, or that any differences are explained and can be allowed for.)
    - ☐ Yes
    - ☐ No

34. Are the registers for persons (PWDs, unemployed, poor) that your office collects, compiles, or consolidates spatially comparable with other economies?
    (Spatial comparability implies that, from economy to economy, the data are based on common concepts, definitions, classifications and methodology, or that any differences are explained and can be allowed for.)
    - ☐ Yes
    - ☐ No

35. Are the registers of farms that your office collects, compiles, or consolidates spatially comparable with other economies?
    (Spatially comparability implies that, from economy to economy, the data are based on common concepts, definitions, classifications and methodology, or that any differences are explained and can be allowed for.)
    - ☐ Yes
    - ☐ No

36. Are the telephone registers that your office collects, compiles, or consolidates spatially comparable with other economies?
    (Spatial comparability implies that, from economy to economy, the data are based on common concepts, definitions, classifications and methodology, or that any differences are explained and can be allowed for.)
    - ☐ Yes
    - ☐ No

37. Are the foreign trade registers that your office collects, compiles, or consolidates spatially comparable with other economies?
(Spatially comparability implies that, from economy to economy, the data are based on common concepts, definitions, classifications and methodology, or that any differences are explained and can be allowed for.)
   ☐ Yes
   ☐ No

38. Are the border records that your office collects, compiles, or consolidates spatially comparable with other economies?
(Spatial comparability implies that, from economy to economy, the data are based on common concepts, definitions, classifications and methodology, or that any differences are explained and can be allowed for.)
   ☐ Yes
   ☐ No

39. Are the business registries that your office collects, compiles, or consolidates spatially comparable with other economies?
(Spatial comparability implies that, from economy to economy, the data are based on common concepts, definitions, classifications and methodology, or that any differences are explained and can be allowed for.)
   ☐ Yes
   ☐ No

40. Are the social security data that your office collects, compiles, or consolidates comparable over time?
(Comparability over time implies that the data are based on common concepts, definitions, and methods over time, or that any differences are explained and can be allowed for.)
   ☐ Yes
   ☐ No

41. Are the health records that your office collects, compiles, or consolidates comparable over time?
(Comparability over time implies that the data are based on common concepts, definitions, and methods over time, or that any differences are explained and can be allowed for.)
   ☐ Yes
   ☐ No

42. Are the education records that your office collects, compiles, or consolidates comparable over time?
(Comparability over time implies that the data are based on common concepts, definitions, and methods over time, or that any differences are explained and can be allowed for.)
   ☐ Yes
   ☐ No

43. Are the registers for persons (PWDs, unemployed, poor) that your office collects, compiles, or consolidates comparable over time?
(Comparability over time implies that the data are based on common concepts, definitions, and methods over time, or that any differences are explained and can be allowed for.)
   ☐ Yes
   ☐ No

44. Are the registers for farms that your office collects, compiles, or consolidates comparable over time? (Comparability over time implies that the data are based on common concepts, definitions, and methods over time, or that any differences are explained and can be allowed for.)
    - ☐ Yes
    - ☐ No

45. Are the telephone registers that your office collects, compiles, or consolidates comparable over time? (Comparability over time implies that the data are based on common concepts, definitions, and methods over time, or that any differences are explained and can be allowed for.)
    - ☐ Yes
    - ☐ No

46. Are the foreign trade registers that your office collects, compiles, or consolidates comparable over time? (Comparability over time implies that the data are based on common concepts, definitions, and methods over time, or that any differences are explained and can be allowed for.)
    - ☐ Yes
    - ☐ No

47. Are the border records that your office collects, compiles, or consolidates comparable over time? (Comparability over time implies that the data are based on common concepts, definitions, and methods over time, or that any differences are explained and can be allowed for.)
    - ☐ Yes
    - ☐ No

48. Are the business registers that your office collects, compiles, or consolidates comparable over time? (Comparability over time implies that the data are based on common concepts, definitions, and methods over time, or that any differences are explained and can be allowed for.)
    - ☐ Yes
    - ☐ No

Part II. COVID-19 Pandemic-Related Experiences on the Collection of Administrative Data

49. What are the impacts of the coronavirus disease (COVID-19) pandemic on your data collection activities? Please check all that apply.
    - ☐ Our data collection activities (e.g., updating of administrative data) have to be rescheduled, postponed, or canceled because of restrictions on movements of people. (*Please proceed to Question 51*)
    - ☐ Our data collection activities (e.g., updating of administrative data) have to be rescheduled, postponed, or canceled to reallocate resources for other COVID-19 pandemic-related response. (*Please proceed to Question 51*)
    - ☐ Our data collection activities (e.g., updating of administrative data.) have resorted to other ways of collecting data. (*Please proceed to Question 50*)
    - ☐ ______________________________________

50. Please specify the other ways of collecting data that your office has resort to.
    ____

51. What specific issues did your office encounter in collecting administrative data during the pandemic?
    Please check all that apply.
    ☐ Administrative data collected by our office are not consolidated in a database-like format.
    ☐ Administrative data is not updated.
    ☐ There are concerns on data quality affecting reliable statistical analysis (e.g., comparability across
      space, time).
    ☐ Incomplete coverage of data (e.g., data available for selected geographical areas or population
      group only).
    ☐ Disruption in office operations because of lockdowns and restrictions.
    ☐ Inadequate access to necessary information technology infrastructure (e.g., for work-from-home
      setup or remote access).
    ☐ Lack of human resources in compilation.
    ☐ Others (please specify) [   ]

Part III. Initiatives to Enhance the Collection and Use of Administrative Data

52. Does your office have plans or initiatives to expand the collection of administrative data to supplement or
    enhance the current data portfolio that your office has?
    ☐ Yes (*Please proceed to Question 53*)
    ☐ No (*Please proceed to Question 57*)

53. Please provide details of your office's plans or initiatives on the expansion of collection of administrative data
    (e.g., innovations in data collection).
    [   ]

54. Proposed date of launch (if not yet launched) or actual date of launch (if already started).
    [   ]

55. Specific purpose of the initiative.
    [   ]

56. Status.
    ☐ Planning stage.
    ☐ Ongoing.
    ☐ Completed.

57. What actions do you propose to improve and strengthen the use of administrative data? Please check all
    that apply.
    ☐ Establish a statistical database or register that is readily accessible to users.
    ☐ Ensure regular updating of administrative data.
    ☐ Improve data quality to allow for reliable statistical analysis (e.g., comparability across space
      and/or time.) (Comparability implies that the data are based on common concepts, definitions,
      and methods across location or over time, or that any differences are explained and can be
      allowed for.)
    ☐ Improve coverage and granularity of data (implies that the data sufficiently represent samples from
      each subgroup of the population or each geographic area).
    ☐ Conduct training on data analytics.
    ☐ Conduct (in house and outsourced) research studies on use of administrative data.

- ☐ Explore innovative dissemination practices (e.g., through social media and other online platforms).
- ☐ Establish more partnerships with other government offices.
- ☐ Simplify data sharing protocols.
- ☐ Strengthen data confidentiality.
- ☐ Others (please specify)

References

S. Akter, et al. 2022. A Gender-Sensitive Earthquake Recovery Assessment Using Administrative and Satellite Data: The Case of Indonesia's 2016 Aceh Earthquake. *ADB Economics Working Paper Series*. No. 674. Manila: Asian Development Bank. https://www.adb.org/sites/default/files/publication/859951/ewp-674-gender-specific-earthquake-recovery-indonesia.pdf.

J. R. Albert and A. Martinez, Jr. 2018. The Future of Data Today. *Development Asia*. Manila: ADB. https://development.asia/explainer/future-data-today.

J. R. Albert, J. D. Monje, and M. S. Muñoz. 2021. SocPen Beyond Ten: A Process Evaluation of the DSWD Social Pension (SocPen) Program for Indigent Senior Citizens amid the COVID-19 Pandemic. *PIDS Discussion Paper Series 2021-31*. Quezon City: Philippine Institute for Development Studies. https://pidswebs.pids.gov.ph/CDN/PUBLICATIONS/pidsdps2131.pdf.

J. R. Albert, et al. 2019. Readiness of National Statistical Systems in Asia and the Pacific for Leveraging Big Data to Monitor the SDGs. *ADB Briefs No. 106*. Manila: Asian Development Bank (ADB). https://www.adb.org/sites/default/files/publication/491326/adb-brief-106-national-statistical-systems-big-data-sdgs.pdf.

Asian Development Bank. 2010. Administrative Data Sources for Compiling Millennium Development Goals and Related Indicators: A Reference Handbook on Using Data from Education, Health, and Vital Registration Systems Featuring Practices and Experiences from Selected Countries. Manila. https://www.adb.org/sites/default/files/publication/28297/sources-compiling-mdg.pdf.

———. 2017. Reforming Social Welfare Programs in Mongolia. ADB Briefs. No. 86. November. Manila. https://www.adb.org/sites/default/files/publication/383161/adb-brief-86.pdf.

———. 2021a. Key Indicators for Asia and the Pacific 2021. (August). https://www.adb.org/sites/default/files/publication/720461/ki2021.pdf.

———. 2021b. Mapping the Spatial Distribution of Poverty Using Satellite Imagery in Thailand. Manila. https://www.adb.org/sites/default/files/publication/695616/mapping-poverty-satellite-imagery-thailand.pdf.

———. 2021c. Practical Guidebook on Data Disaggregation for the Sustainable Development Goals. Manila (May). https://www.adb.org/sites/default/files/publication/698116/guidebook-data-disaggregation-sdgs.pdf.

———. 2022a. Key Indicators for Asia and the Pacific 2022. https://www.adb.org/publications/key-indicators-asia-and-pacific-2022.

———. 2022b. Mongolia: Building Capacity for an Effective Social Welfare System. Consultant's report. Manila (TA 9893-MON). https://www.adb.org/sites/default/files/project-documents/51387/51387-001-tacr-en_1.pdf.

———. 2022c. Survey on the Use of Administrative Data for the Compilation of Employment-Related Indicators.

Australian Aid and United Nations Population Fund, Asia and the Pacific Regional Office. 2020. *kNowVAWdata—Administrative data systems versus prevalence surveys: Are they equally suited to give us data on the prevalence of violence against women?* Bangkok. https://asiapacific.unfpa.org/sites/default/files/pub-pdf/vaw-sources-of-data-28august2020-final.pdf.

Australian Bureau of Statistics (ABS). Administrative data snapshot of population and housing. https://www.abs.gov.au/about/data-services/data-integration/integrated-data/administrative-data-snapshot-population-and-housing.

G. J. Brackstone. 1999. Managing data quality in a statistical agency. *Survey Methodology*. 25 (2). Catalogue No. 12-001. pp. 139–149. Ottawa: Statistics Canada. https://www150.statcan.gc.ca/n1/en/pub/12-001-x/1999002/article/4877-eng.pdf?st=NKWj1vK0.

Data2X. 2019. Measuring women's paid and unpaid work under ICLS 19. *Policymaker's brief.* https://data2x.org/wp-content/uploads/2019/08/PolicyMakerBrief_Online-WR-181003.pdf.

Government of Canada, Statistics Canada. Request for information – Labour. https://www.statcan.gc.ca/en/our-data/where/admin-rfi/labour#Employment-insurance-social-assistance.

Government of New Zealand, Statistics New Zealand. Data integration projects and privacy impact assessments. https://web.archive.org/web/20190122153642/ http:/archive.stats.govt.nz/methods/data-integration/data-integration-projects.aspx.

Government of the Philippines, Department of Labor and Employment. 2020. Prescribing Guidelines on the Provision of Financial Assistance for Displaced Landbased and Seabased Filipino Workers Due to the Corona Virus (COVID-2019) "DOLE-AKAP for OFWs". *Department Order*. No. 212. Manila. https://www.dole.gov.ph/news/department-order-no-212-series-of-2020-prescribing-guidelines-on-the-provision-of-financial-assistance-for-displaced-landbased-and-seabased-filipino-workers-due-to-the-corona-virus-covid-2019-d/.

Government of the Republic of Korea. 2007, as amended from time to time. Statistics Act. https://elaw.klri.re.kr/eng_mobile/viewer.do?hseq=44517&type=part&key=19.

Government of Tonga. 2016. Statistics Act: 2016 Revised Edition. https://ago.gov.to/cms/images/LEGISLATION/PRINCIPAL/2015/2015-0007/StatisticsAct_2.pdf.

R. Hayashi, N. Matsuda, and M. S. Rahman. 2022. Online Job Listings Rebounded Strongly After the Pandemic. *Asian Development Blog*. July. Manila: ADB. https://blogs.adb.org/blog/online-job-listings-rebounded-strongly-after-pandemic.

International Labour Organization (ILO). 2017. *Quick Guide on Sources and Uses of Labour Statistics*. Geneva. https://www.ilo.org/wcmsp5/groups/public/---dgreports/---stat/documents/publication/wcms_590092.pdf.

———. 2017. Decent work for sustainable development Resource Platform: Indicators for Gender Equality and Non-Discrimination. https://www.ilo.org/global/topics/dw4sd/themes/gender-equality/WCMS_560718/lang--en/index.htm.

———. 2017. Decent work for sustainable development Resource Platform: Gender Equality and Non-Discrimination. https://www.ilo.org/global/topics/dw4sd/themes/gender-equality/lang--en/index.htm.

———. Decent work for sustainable development Resource Platform: Thematic areas. https://www.ilo.org/global/topics/dw4sd/themes/lang--en/index.htm.

———. Decent work for sustainable development Resource Platform: Policy Outcomes. https://www.ilo.org/global/topics/dw4sd/theme-by-policy-outcomes/lang--en/index.htm.

———. 2022. Quick guide to understanding the impact of the new statistical standards on ILOSTAT Databases. Geneva. https://www.ilo.org/wcmsp5/groups/public/---dgreports/---stat/documents/publication/wcms_854830.pdf.

ILO/ East Asia Multidisciplinary Advisory Team. 1997. *Labour statistics based on administrative records: Guidelines on compilation and presentation*. Bangkok: ILO Regional Office for Asia and the Pacific. https://www.ilo.org/public/libdoc/ilo/1997/97B09_105_engl.pdf.

K. Kõiv, et al. 2018. Profile of effective NEET-youth support service. Erasmus+ Strategic Partnership project "Community Guarantee" 2017-1-EE01-KA205-034723. Põltsamaa, Estonia: Association of Estonian Open Youth Centres. https://ank.ee/wp-content/uploads/2018/10/CommunityGuarantee.IO1_.Final_.pdf.

J. Lee and M. Kang. 2015. Geospatial Big Data: Challenges and Opportunities. *Big Data Research*. Volume 2, Issue 2, pp. 74-81. https://doi.org/10.1016/j.bdr.2015.01.003.

London School of Economics and Political Science, United Nations Statistics Division, and the Global Partnership for Sustainable Development Data. 2021. *Re-using Administrative Data for Statistics: Case Studies from Five Countries*. New York.

A. Martinez, et al. 2018. Big Data Can Transform SDG Performance. Here's How. *Asian Development Blog*. June. Manila: ADB. https://blogs.adb.org/blog/big-data-can-transform-sdg-performance-here-s-how.

C. Martinez-Fernandez and M. Powell. 2010. Employment and Skills Strategies in Southeast Asia: Setting the Scene. *OECD Local Economic and Employment Development (LEED) Papers*. No. 2010/01Paris: OECD Publishing. https://doi.org/10.1787/5kmbjglh34r5-en.

D. Mirdamadi. 2022. Geospatial Technology: Applications and Benefits. https://mgiss.co.uk/geospatial-technology-applications-and-benefits/.

———. Integrated Data Infrastructure. https://www.digital.govt.nz/showcase/integrated-data-tools/.

———. Longitudinal Business Database. https://www.stats.govt.nz/integrated-data/longitudinal-business-database/.

———. De-identified data fact sheet – *supporting analytical insights while maintaining privacy and confidentiality*. Wellington. https://www.stats.govt.nz/assets/Uploads/Integrated-data-infrastructure/de-identified-data -supporting-analytical-insights-while-maintaining-privacy-and-confidentiality.pdf.

———. Data integration projects and privacy impact assessments. https://web.archive.org/web/20190122153642/ http:/archive.stats.govt.nz/methods/data-integration/data-integration-projects.aspx.

Organisation for Economic Co-operation and Development (OECD). 2017. OECD Handbook for Internationally Comparative Education Statistics: Concepts, Standards, Definitions and Classifications. Paris. http://dx.doi .org/10.1787/9789264279889-en.

———. 2021. Improving the Provision of Active Labour Market Policies in Estonia, Connecting People with Jobs, OECD Publishing, Paris, https://doi.org/10.1787/31f72c5b-en.

R.J. Pember. 1998. *Compilation and Presentation of Labour Statistics Based on Administrative Records*. January. Geneva: ILO. https://www.ilo.org/wcmsp5/groups/public/---dgreports/---stat/documents/publication/ wcms_087895.pdf.

Philippine Statistics Authority. 2012. 2010 Census of Population and Housing. Manila (Table 4). https://psa.gov .ph/system/files/phcd/2022-12/Table4_9.pdf.

F.C. Soco, et al. 2021a. Harnessing Administrative Data for Evidence-Based Policy-Making. Development Asia. *Development Asia.* Manila: https://development.asia/insight/harnessing-administrative-data-evidence -based-labor-policy-making.

F.C. Soco, et al. 2021b. Preparing a Road Map on the Use of Administrative Data for Compiling Employment Statistics. *ADB Briefs. No. 179*. Manila, ADB. https://www.adb.org/sites/default/files/publication/705846/ adb-brief-179-administrative-data-employment-statistics.pdf.

United Nations Economic Commission for Europe (UNECE). 2020. *Guidance on the Use of Longitudinal Data for Migration Statistics*. Geneva: UNECE. https://unece.org/sites/default/files/2021-03/ECECESSTAT20206.pdf.

———. 2018. *Guidelines on the Use of Registers and Administrative Data for Population and Housing Censuses*. Geneva: UNECE. https://unece.org/DAM/stats/publications/2018/ECECESSTAT20184.pdf.

———. 2011. *Using Administrative and Secondary Sources for Official Statistics: A Handbook of Principles and Practices*. Geneva: UNECE. https://unece.org/statistics/mos/using-administrative-and-secondary-sources -official-statistics.

———. 2007. Register-based statistics in the Nordic Countries: Review of the best practices with focus on population and social statistics. Geneva: UNECE. https://unstats.un.org/unsd/dnss/docViewer.aspx?docID=2764.

United Nations Economic and Social Commission for Asia and the Pacific (UNESCAP). 2022. Tapping into administrative data in census-taking: an emerging trend in Asia and the Pacific. *Stats Brief*. No. 31. Bangkok. https://repository.unescap.org/bitstream/handle/20.500.12870/4354/ESCAP-2022-PB-Tapping-into -administrative-data-census-taking.pdf?sequence=1&isAllowed=y.

———. 2020. *Asia-Pacific Guidelines to Data Integration for Official Statistics*. Bangkok. https://www.unescap.org/sites/default/d8files/knowledge-products/Data_Integration_Guidelines_ESCAP.pdf.

———. 2019. Asia And The Pacific SDG Progress Report 2019. BangkokPart III: SDG Data Sources and Gaps. https://www.unescap.org/sites/default/files/publications/ESCAP_Asia_and_the_Pacific_SDG_Progress _Report_2019.pdf.

United Nations Statistics Division (UNSD) and the Global Partnership for Sustainable Development Data (GPSDD). Collaborative on the Use of Administrative Data for Statistics. https://unstats.un.org/capacity -development/admin-data/.

———. Collaborative on the Use of Administrative Data for Statistics: Blogs. https://unstats.un.org/ UNSDWebsite/capacity-development/admin-data/blog/.

———. Collaborative on the Use of Administrative Data for Statistics: Expert Clinics. https://unstats.un.org/ UNSDWebsite/capacity-development/admin-data/clinic/.

———. Collaborative on Use of Administrative Data for Statistics: Webinars and Events. https://unstats.un.org/ UNSDWebsite/capacity-development/admin-data/webinar/.

———. Inventory listing. https://unstats.un.org/UNSDWebsite/capacity-development/admin-data/Inventory.

UNSD. Advances in Strengthening Administrative Data for Official Statistics. Side Event at the 54th session of the United Nations Statistical Commission. https://unstats.un.org/UNSDWebsite/events-details/un54sc -27022023-strengthening-administrative-data.

———. 2022. *Handbook on Management and Organization of National Statistical Systems*. New York. Chapter 8.3. https://unstats.un.org/capacity-development/handbook/html/topic.htm#t=Handbook%2FC8%2FAdminis trative_sources.htm.

———. Mapping of SDG Global Indicators to Household Sample Surveys. https://unstats.un.org/unsd/ statcom/49th-session/documents/BG-Item3d-Mapping-of-Household-Surveys-to-Global-SDG -indicators-E.xlsx (accessed 24 August 2023).

———. SDG Global Database. https://unstats.un.org/sdgs/dataportal/database (accessed 22 December 2022).

———. SDG Indicators: Metadata Repository. https://unstats.un.org/sdgs/metadata/ (accessed 14 December 2022).

———. 2021. *Case Study- Colombia. Labour market perspectives from the statistical register of labour relations*. New York. https://unstats.un.org/capacity-development/admin-data/DetailedView/60d9ed2b63e8753688667ce9.

———. 2021. Expert clinic on interoperability and data linking. https://unstats.un.org/UNSDWebsite/capacity -development/admin-data/clinic3/.

———. 2021. Expert clinic on labour statistics. https://unstats.un.org/UNSDWebsite/capacity-development/ admin-data/clinic1/.

———. 2018. Use of administrative data for official statistics: The Global Perspective. Presented in the International Workshop on Sustainable Development Goal Indicators, 27 June 2018 in Beijing, China. https://unstats.un.org/sdgs/files/meetings/sdg-inter-workshop-june-2018/Day2_Session3_Adm%20 Data_UNSD.pdf.

www.ingramcontent.com/pod-product-compliance
Lightning Source LLC
LaVergne TN
LVHW071451180726
843512LV00018B/1346